DARWINISM, DOMINANCE, AND DEMOCRACY

DARWINISM, DOMINANCE, AND DEMOCRACY

The Biological Bases
of Authoritarianism

**Albert Somit
and Steven A. Peterson**

Human Evolution, Behavior, and Intelligence
Seymour W. Itzkoff, Series Editor

**Westport, Connecticut
London**

Library of Congress Cataloging-in-Publication Data

Somit, Albert.
    Darwinism, dominance, and democracy : the biological bases of
authoritarianism / Albert Somit and Steven A. Peterson.
        p.   cm.— (Human evolution, behavior, and intelligence, ISSN
1063–2158)
    Includes bibliographical references and index.
    ISBN 0–275–95817–5 (alk. paper)
    1. Biopolitics. 2. Social Darwinism. 3. Authoritarianism.
4. Democracy. I. Peterson, Steven A. II. Title. III. Series.
JA80.S596   1997
321.8′01—dc20   96–36359

British Library Cataloguing in Publication Data is available.

Library of Congress Catalog Card Number: 96–36359
ISBN: 0–275–95817–5
ISSN: 1063–2158

First published in 1997

Praeger Publishers, 88 Post Road West, Westport, CT 06881
An imprint of Greenwood Publishing Group, Inc.

Printed in the United States of America

The paper used in this book complies with the
Permanent Paper Standard issued by the National
Information Standards Organization (Z39.48–1984).

10 9 8 7 6 5 4 3 2 1

To Joe Tanenhaus—"a loss so great"

To Evan Franzese-Peterson—looking toward the future

Contents

Acknowledgments

For invaluable logistical support, we thank Christine Grontkowski, Dean of the College of Liberal Arts and Sciences at Alfred University; John H. Jackson, College of Liberal Arts and Sciences, Southern Illinois University; and the Department of Political Science, Southern Illinois University. For sagacious advice and counsel, we are indebted to Professor William E. Eaton, Southern Illinois University; Dr. Malcolm Litchfield, Princeton University Press; Professor Lionel Tiger, Rutgers University; and Mr. Thomas C. Wallace, Wallace Literary Agency. And we are grateful to Mr. Robert Quarteroni, former Director of Public Relations at Alfred University (and currently at Montclair State), for expert professional assistance above and beyond the call of institutional duty.

None of these individuals, we hasten to add, necessarily shares the opinions and views expressed in this book.

Part I

Introduction

Chapter 1

Prologue to a Predictably Unpopular Thesis

The danger is not that of being refuted, but of being misunderstood.
Immanuel Kant, *Critique of Pure Reason*, 1927 trans.

This book seeks to explain an incontrovertible though hardly welcome fact: Throughout human history, the overwhelming majority of political societies have been characterized by the rule of the few over the many, by dominance and submission, by command and obedience.

No matter the century or era, we see the same pattern—authoritarian regimes are notable by their presence and persistence, democracies by their infrequency and impermanence. This has unarguably been the case in the past; an objective assessment of today's some two hundred polities compels the conclusion that, even in what is hailed as an "Age of Democracy," it still remains essentially the case today.[1]

The consistency of this pattern raises two very troublesome questions. First and most obvious: Why are authoritarian governments so common and enduring—and democracies, in painful contrast, so rare and, all too often, so fragile? To this question, many answers have been offered; as their sheer number and variety testifies, none has yet been particularly persuasive.

In this book we address the same issue but advance a quite different explanation. Although other factors are undoubtedly also operative, the most important reason for the rarity of democracy is that evolution has endowed our species, as it has the other social primates, with a predisposition for hierarchically structured social and political systems. In the pages that follow, we will try both to explain why and how this has occurred and, equally important, to anticipate the objections that likely will (and certainly should) be raised to such an unattractive thesis.

The proposed explanation promptly triggers the second question: How, then, can we account for the undeniable occasional emergence of democratic polities? Many of those who have wrestled with this problem find the answer in some unique concatenation of economic, social, historical, and political "facilitating" factors. These factors undoubtedly play a role. Nonetheless, paradoxically enough, we must again turn to evolutionary theory for the necessary, though not sufficient, condition that makes democracy sometimes possible.

Although it shares the proclivity of its fellow social primates for hierarchical social organization, Homo sapiens is the only species capable of creating and, under some circumstances, acting in accordance with cultural beliefs that actually run *counter* to its innate behavioral tendencies. The generally accepted, if lamentably awkward, term for this truly unique capacity is "indoctrinability."[2] Celibacy and the (presumably) less demanding ideal of faithful monogamy are obvious examples of indoctrinability at work. Democracy, an idea almost as alien to our social primate nature, is another. It is indoctrinability, then, that makes it possible, given some conjunction of the aforementioned facilitating social, economic, and other, conditions, for democracies occasionally to emerge and to have some chance to survive.

Our original objective was to address the two questions identified above. As we proceeded, however, a third task emerged. A neo-Darwinian perspective on the prospects of democracy in a social primate species can all too easily be misperceived as deliberately or inadvertently (the net effect is the same) antidemocratic in thrust. That is assuredly neither our position nor our desire. Our intent, rather, is to show that the democratic cause will continue to be ill served if we fail to take adequate account of our species' innate hierarchical inclinations.

That evolution has endowed Homo sapiens with a genetic bias toward hierarchy, dominance, and submission need not necessarily be a counsel of despair. Better to grasp this reality[3] than to blissfully believe that our species is innately democratic in its political tendencies and that other forms of government are unfortunate, but essentially temporary, aberrations. Only after we recognize and accept that fact can we begin to think realistically about the type of domestic and foreign policies required for the survival of democratic government, a subject to which we finally decided to devote our concluding chapter.

Failing a basic evolutionary understanding, there is little reason to expect that democracies will be any more common or viable in the future than they have been in the past or are in the world around us today. Unless we both comprehend and act on that understanding, democracy risks the fate that inevitably undertakes almost all endangered species—extinction.

This thesis, we realize, will be neither popular nor readily accepted. As Robert Wright has lately remarked (1994:5):

The new Darwinian social scientists are fighting a doctrine which has dominated their fields for much of this century: the idea that biology doesn't much matter—that the uniquely malleable human mind, together with the unique force of culture, has severed our inherent human nature from its evolutionary roots.

Readers who completely reject the concept of evolution, whether neo-Darwinian, Lamarckian, or other, are not likely to proceed beyond this point. In fact, we fear, they have already taken their leave. Those who accept evolution in principle but deny its applicability to humans[4] will, we hope, persist a bit longer. It is to them and to those who, however reluctantly, are willing to consider the possibility that biology might have some influence on human political behavior that this book is addressed.

One last preliminary comment: Normally, it is a marked advantage to write a book aimed at an English-speaking audience, given the size, comparative educational level, and relative affluence of that prospective readership. In this case, though, it may well be a serious disadvantage. The reason is quite simple: The great majority of those for whom English is their mother tongue were born and raised in democracies—that is, Australia, Canada, Great Britain, the United States, and New Zealand. For most of them, democracy is the natural mode of governance and constitutes the totality of their firsthand political experience. That experience very often makes it difficult, if not impossible, for them to realize how unusual democracies are in the family of polities. And it almost surely predisposes them to reject out of hand the idea that we, as a species, are otherwise politically inclined. For many of our readers, even those who accept the validity of neo-Darwinian thought, this will indeed be, as the phrase goes, a truly tough sell.

NOTES

1. Chapter 4 documents this contention in considerable detail. Perhaps the best that one can say is that democracies are currently slightly less *un*common than in previous centuries.

2. More formally stated, the term refers to "the routines and practices that individuals use to instill or to maintain in themselves [or in others] an aspirational identity" (Caton, 1995:6).

3. As Dawkins has put it (1989b:3): "if you wish to build a society in which individuals cooperate generously and unselfishly toward a common good, you can expect little help from biological nature."

4. "Even with the rationality that is part of being human, we find it difficult . . . to attach ourselves through an unbroken chain of genetic inheritance to the simian world" (Leakey and Lewin, 1992:80). They later remark that "many people believe that humans are so different from the rest of the animal world, they cannot accept the idea that we are a product of evolution" (1992:199).

Chapter 2

Darwinism and Democracy: The Problem of the Missing Polity

Humans worldwide belong to one species, Homo sapiens, the
product of a particular evolutionary history.
    Richard Leakey and Roger Lewin, *Origins Reconsidered*, 1992

FROM ROUSSEAU TO REALITY

Few passages in political philosophy are better known than the opening
sentences of Rousseau's *Social Contract*. With characteristic confidence in
his own judgment, he proclaims that "man is born free but is everywhere in
chains. How did this come about? That I do not know. What can make it
legitimate? That I believe I can explain."

Regrettably, Rousseau was wrong, dead wrong. We are *not* born free. On
the contrary, we come into the world bearing the shackles of our evolutionary past. What can make this legitimate? That, alas, we do not know. How
did this come about? That, we believe, we can now explain.

As 6,000 or so years of recorded history testify, from the emergence of
the "state" to the present, the vast majority of mankind have lived under one
form or another (the descriptive terms vary, the essence remains much the
same) of authoritarian rule. Democracies have been notably rare; most have
been endangered almost from the moment of their birth; most have been
depressingly short-lived.

Why, to repeat, have authoritarian governments been so much the rule
and democracies so much the exception? A variety of factors, varying from
one country to another, have indubitably been operative. But taking the

record as a whole, we think it fair to say, neo-Darwinian theory offers the single most powerful and intellectually coherent explanation.

Humans are social primates, closely (almost embarrassingly) akin genetically to the chimpanzees and only slightly less so to the gorillas. Working over at least 10 million years, natural selection has endowed the social primates with a "predisposition" (to understate the matter) for hierarchical social structures. That is, they invariably form groups, troops, tribes, and societies characterized by marked differences in individual status in terms of dominance and submission, command and obedience, and by unequal access to many of the good things of life.

These hierarchically organized modes of existence evolved among all the social primates, varying only in detail from one species to another. They evolved because they contributed significantly, on balance, to the "inclusive fitness"[1] of the individual member, whether male or female, dominant or subordinate. Dominance and submission, and so forth, became integral aspects of the genetically transmitted behavioral repertoire of the social primates because they served an important, perhaps nearly indispensable, evolutionary function.

But in nature as elsewhere, there is no free lunch. This genetic legacy has left Homo sapiens with an innate bias toward authoritarian, that is, hierarchical, political and social systems. In short, the single most important reason for the relative rarity of democratic government is to be found not in our stars but in our genes.[2]

At this juncture, two objections should come to mind. If we are by nature inherently antidemocratic, why is it that, as Sartori (1965) ironically observed, the name "democracy" is now so sacred that nobody now dares to say that he is antidemocratic? Or, to put the question in slightly different form, why is it that with very few exceptions,[3] the most despotic and authoritarian governments unabashedly claim the term "democracy," if often with some modifying adjective, for their regimes?

The answer is threefold. First, of course, we should remember that the popularity of democracy, in the traditional sense of "one man, one vote," is a fairly recent political phenomenon, dating back barely 150 years. Before that, as we will see, "democracy" was commonly used as a term of opprobrium. Second, from Plato to the present, none of our great political philosophers—no, not even Rousseau[4] or John Stuart Mill[5]—has been other than rather skeptical, to put it charitably, about the merits of democratic governance.

Third, and probably most important, the present popular appeal of the term in large part springs from the strikingly diverse and often contradictory uses, as Alexis de Tocqueville presciently warned,[6] to which it has been put.

There can be no better examples of this than the insistence of the (now defunct) USSR and (at this writing, still viable) North Korean and mainland Chinese governments that they were or are a "people's democracy." Or, to take a hardly less egregious instance, the American government's announced determination, in 1994, to "restore democracy in Haiti." When, we may wonder, have the unfortunate Haitians ever had a government that even remotely resembled a democracy?

There remains, to be sure, a second major objection. How is it that some democracies do appear from time to time and that, happily, some do survive? There were, after all, maybe fifty glorious democratic years in Athens and, after a lengthy interval, a century or so of democratic grandeur in Rome. Then, after a hiatus of more than a millennium and a half, there once again emerged another democracy. And today, of the nearly two hundred states that comprise the United Nations, there are possibly two score (see chapter 4) that merit this designation. Given our basic thesis, how do we account for even this modest minority of democratic polities?

Many social scientists have sought to identify the conditions that make democracy sometimes viable. A few believe that this is probably a random event, similar perhaps to a meteor somehow surviving its journey through the atmosphere and eventually managing to strike the earth. Most of those who have addressed this question, though, find the answer in some special concatenation of social, economic, historical, and political factors (frequently referred to as "enabling" conditions).

These factors, as we note in chapter 3, undoubtedly play a role. Nonetheless, paradoxically enough, we must again turn to evolutionary theory for a better understanding of what makes democracy occasionally possible.

A neo-Darwinian approach holds that Homo sapiens share the social primate proclivity for hierarchical social organization, but this approach also emphasizes that mankind has evolved some behavioral attributes and capacities that are, in effect, unique in the animal kingdom.

There has been, of course, a long-running debate over whether other primate species are capable of language or, to take another controversy, of self-consciousness. Agreement on these matters has yet to be achieved. There is near unanimity, though, that Homo sapiens alone have attained the intellectual level required to create, in more than very rudimentary form,[7] that vast complex of language, laws, customs and mores, art forms, material objects, technology, ideas and values subsumed by the term "culture."

The chasm between Homo sapiens and the other primates has been graphically described by Robin Fox (1989:28):

Man is different from other primates, not because he has in some way *overcome* his primate nature, but because he is a different kind of primate with a different kind of nature. . . . [M]an behaves culturally, because mutation and natural selection have produced an animal that *must* behave culturally—invent rules, make myths, speak languages, and form men's clubs, in the same way as the hamadryas baboon must form harems, adopt infants, and bite his wives on the neck.

Some of the ideas and values that constitute so large a component of any people's culture are often attributed to a divine source; other ideas and values, especially those of a more secular character, have unmistakably human origins. Whatever their putative inspiration, these ideas and values, once brought into existence, are capable of profoundly altering the behaviors of those who believe in them.[8] This remarkable trait, manifested only by our own species, is what we have previously referred to as indoctrinability.

When this occurs, humankind literally becomes the servant of its own creations;[9] in some instances, culture may even triumph, at least temporarily, over nature. True believers often willingly undertake actions and pursue goals that may be strikingly different from those to which our evolutionary history has otherwise predisposed us.

Religion offers the most familiar example of indoctrinability. Left to its own untutored impulses, mankind is all too prone to engage, for example, in sex, aggression, and violence. Painfully cognizant of the enthusiastic readiness with which we pursue these activities, almost all religious codes strive earnestly to prohibit, or at least discourage, them.

Thus, almost all religions urge—or command—their followers to be chaste, if not celibate; not to become overly enamored of worldly possessions; to share with the poor; to forgive those who offend them; to be properly humble; even to love their neighbors as they love themselves. Granted, these commandments are not invariably obeyed. Nonetheless, religions have long demonstrated their ability to modify, sometimes drastically, sometimes only partially and transiently, the behaviors of their adherents. And, we might add, to evoke feelings of guilt—and thus possibly influence the future behavior—of those who transgress their teachings.

But religious beliefs are not the only source of behavior that literally run against the biological grain. Secular doctrines no less than theological teachings have the same remarkable power. As repeatedly demonstrated over the centuries, social and political ideologies can also sometimes inspire their adherents to engage in actions and to pursue objectives that are at great variance from those to which their primate evolutionary legacy would otherwise incline them.[10]

So, from time to time, and for reasons that differ from situation to situation, "democratic" ideas may gain acceptance among some sizable and/or influential segment of a nation's population. If this occurs in conjunction with certain of the previously mentioned social, economic, and other, conditions, then and then only does a viable democracy become possible. Lamentably, it is not a conjunction that occurs very often.

This view of the matter suggests that perhaps another widely accepted idea should be turned on its head. The commonsense understanding is that the post–World War I triumphs of national socialism and fascism in Italy and Germany and the subsequent post–World War II sweep of totalitarian Marxism in Eastern Europe and elsewhere were to be explained in substantial part as the victory of clever totalitarian propaganda—that is, of effective indoctrination—over mankind's "natural" democratic preference.

A contrary understanding may be closer to what actually occurred. By virtue of its genetic makeup, mankind may resonate much more readily to elitist and authoritarian ideologies. Accordingly, propaganda and indoctrination may account more plausibly for the occasional emergence of democracy than for the acceptance achieved by authoritarian modes of rule.[11]

To summarize: There is undoubtedly some validity to the notion that democracy demands certain material preconditions. But this familiar formulation overlooks the single most important requirement of all: For a democracy to be born and to survive also demands that nurture, in the sense of a compelling ideological conviction, triumph over nature, that is, our inherent primate predisposition for hierarchical social and authoritarian political systems. It is this second requirement, we suggest, that not only explains democracy's occasional appearance but accounts for its infrequency, its frailty and, so often, its brief life span.

ORGANIZATION OF THE VOLUME

That, in summary fashion, is the case we seek to make. The next task, of course, is that of presenting the argument in more detailed and, we hope, convincingly documented fashion.

Part 2 ("Democracy as *Rara Avis*: The Empirical Evidence") of this book is designed to validate our contention that both in the historical past and, more to the point, even now, after two world wars fought (one explicitly and the other implicitly) to make the world safe for democracy, such governments have been and still remain very much in the minority.

Democracies constitute a small minority of past and present polities—but they do exist. What makes this possible? In chapter 3 ("Prerequisites of Democracy: Necessary but Not Quite Sufficient") we review the various answers offered to this question. By and large, most students agree, democracy requires some combination of social, economic, and political enabling conditions, the exact nature of this combination as yet unknown. We agree. Still, as the title of the chapter indicates, we do not regard these conditions as sufficient in themselves to overcome our inherent authoritarian proclivities. For that to occur, as we will later seek to show, indoctrinablity must also be operative.

One key focus of this part of the volume is an agreement on the basic features of a democratic state. Accordingly, at the outset of chapter 4 ("Will the Real Democracies Please Stand Up") we propose a widely utilized "soft" definition that very few persons, we are confident, will regard as overly demanding. In the balance of this chapter, we (1) apply the resulting criteria to the historical span running from circa 3500 B.C.E. to circa mid-nineteenth century; then (2) in what is manifestly a critical test, we look at the presence and absence of democratic polities in our own era—so often heralded as "The Age of Democracy." We do this on literally a country-by-country basis, thus enabling our readers to judge for themselves.

Part 3 ("The Neo-Darwinian Case and Supporting Evidence") presents the evolutionary theory, and the supporting evidence, for the contention that its primate origins has left our species strongly predisposed toward hierarchical social and political structures. We discuss here the reproductive advantages of hierarchy, dominance, obedience and indoctrinability to the individual members of a social species and possibly to the group as well. That is, we consider *why* these behaviors would have evolved in a social species. Those for whom the neo-Darwinian perspective is an unfamiliar way of looking at the world may find it both unsettling and unattractive, since the resulting conclusions sometimes run counter to some of our most cherished political and moral values.

Chapter 5 describes how essentially similar selective pressures have produced much the same basic behaviors—dominance and hierarchy—among all the social primates, although these behaviors vary somewhat from species to species, sometimes even within a species, depending upon the ecological setting. Chapter 6, which focuses on obedience, begins with the overwhelming evidence from real life and then provides further—and sometimes profoundly disturbing—evidence from laboratory experiments dealing with conformity and obedience. Chapter 7, which deals with indoctrinability, traces the probable evolutionary origins and benefits of this unique human trait, one that makes it possible for nurture to triumph over nature from time to time and, by so doing, to make democracy occasionally possible. In these three chapters we draw upon, inter alia, anthropology, sociology, social psychology, utopian history, ethology, primatology, and organizational theory, as well as upon neo-Darwinism, to document our case.

"Democracy" is now so popular a catchphrase that few realize that, until quite recently, it was an unwanted and unloved orphan in the family of political theories. As we note in chapter 8 ("Democratic Philosophy: From Ugly Duckling to Irresistible Swan"), from Plato onward our great philosophers, no matter their other differences, have been united in their distaste for democratic government. Their unanimity on this score, together with a parallel popular antipathy toward democracy until almost the mid-nineteenth century, could reasonably be viewed as further evidence of our species' inherent antidemocratic bias.

Chapter 8 traces the transformation of democracy from a near pariah among political doctrines to being, in the words of a UNESCO (1951) study, "the single most favored ideology today." That transformation is a classic instance of the ability of indoctrinability to overcome an inherent bias or tendency, a triumph greatly facilitated by the many and often contradictory senses in which the term soon came to be used.

That humans are more inclined to authoritarian than democratic governance is not intended as a doomsday declaration. To the contrary: once we are aware of and understand our innate propensities, then and only then can we begin to think realistically about how they might best be offset and countered. In the final analysis, the possibility of utilizing that understanding to strengthen the democratic prospect may constitute the ultimate justification for this book. As one of the leading advocates of a Darwinian approach to human behavior reminded his readers,

If the bearers of bad news have any hope to offer, it is that by facing the unpalatable truths we are better off than if we ignored them. . . . For even if mankind cannot achieve perfection, it can perhaps learn to live more tolerantly with its imperfections. (Fox, 1989:4)

With this objective in mind, part 4 (constituted of one long chapter), examines the implications of an evolutionary perspective for the formulation of public policy. If they are to be successful, policies aimed at strengthening democracy at home and abroad must be based on a realistic understanding of our species' innate behavioral predilections. We sketch the outlines of policies so conceived—and how they would significantly differ, in objective and content, from those that have too often been pursued in the past.

Some of these recommendations, we fear, will be no more popular than our basic thesis. That, though, is to be expected, since they are predicated on the soundness of that thesis.

NOTES

1. Roughly, but not exactly, akin to "reproductive fitness." See chapter 5 for a more detailed treatment.

2. This is perhaps the best place to take cognizance of E. W. Sinnott's "The Biological Basis of Democracy" (1945) written near, and plainly influenced by, the close of World War II. Sinnott argued, as his title indicates, that mankind is by nature democratically inclined. His argument rested on the major premise that mankind is by nature "diverse"; and the minor premise that the "fullest expression of diversity requires freedom," thus leading to the conclusion that humankind thereby seeks freedom. Not surprisingly, Sinnott also saw history as leading inexorably to "progress" and "individuality."

3. The policies of the government of Singapore and similar regimes led *The Economist* to comment on "the general pattern of resistance by [some] Asian leaders to notions about democracy and individual freedoms that most people in the West take as self-evident truths" (Feb. 15, 1992, p. 36).

4. "Taking the word democracy in its strict sense, perhaps there never did, and never will, exist such a government. *It is against the natural order that the greater number should govern, and the smaller number be governed.*" (1973, bk. 3, chap. iv; italics added)

5. Mill, rightly regarded as the major spokesman for representative government, had serious reservations about the wisdom of universal suffrage.

6. "It is our way of using the words 'democracy' and 'democratic government' that brings about the greatest confusion. Unless these words are clearly defined and their definition agreed upon, people will live in an inextricable confusion of ideas, much to the advantage of demagogues and despots" (1945 ed., p. 557).

7. For recent opinion on this matter, see W. C. McGrew, "Chimpanzee Material Culture: What Are Its Limits and Why," in Foley (1991:15–24).

8. "Belief of this kind has two essential prerequisites. First, a high level of language competence. . . . Secondly, a conscious high level use of explanation based on causal theory, i.e., the belief that one event causes another. . . . Both these requirements and particularly their combination make it unlikely that we shall find belief in this form in non-human species" (Premack, in Byrne and Whiten, 1988:174). Darwin himself, as Wright (1994:185) remarks, had suggested that the word "moral" be reserved for Homo sapiens alone.

9. As the Gnostic "Gospel of Philip" puts it, "That is the way it is in the world—human beings make gods, and worship their creation" (Pagels, 1979: 122).

10. Just as they have been willing to sacrifice, suffer, and die for their God, so men and women have been equally ready to give of themselves for flag and country, for one political "ism" or another.

11. Fascism and national socialism were toppled, it should be kept in mind, not by domestic discontent but by external armies; the Stalinist regimes fell not because they were authoritarian but because they were so badly run that they could no longer deliver even the basic necessities required for anything approaching an acceptable standard of life.

Part II

Democracy as *Rara Avis:*
The Empirical Evidence

Chapter 3

Prerequisites of Democracy: Necessary but Not Quite Sufficient

INTRODUCTION

In the next chapter we advance and endorse a widely utilized "soft" definition of democracy. A "real" democracy, it is generally agreed, has two basic characteristics: first, something akin to universal suffrage and majority rule via free competitive elections;[1] second, what is customarily called the "rule of law," that is, the effective protection of civil and political rights by a reasonably independent judiciary.

Our basic thesis is that nature has endowed our species with an innate tendency toward authoritarian rather than democratic governmental (and social) systems. If that is so, the obvious query arises: How can we account for the occasional appearance and survival of democracies both in the past and in the world today?

As a sizeable literature testifies, we are hardly the first to raise this question. Almost everyone who has wrestled with the issue has sought to identify the key prerequisite or enabling conditions for democratic governance. In this chapter, we briefly review these previous attempts, identify the most widely agreed upon requirements, and discuss these under two broad categories, internal requisites and external requisites.

These internal and external conditions are undoubtedly essential; there are very few, if any, instances in which a viable democracy has emerged in their absence. But, as history has shown, their existence *of itself* does not automatically predict, let along ensure, a democratic polity. They are, to borrow a familiar phrase, necessary but not sufficient conditions. There is an additional fundamental (also necessary but not sufficient) requirement that has been almost completely ignored in the traditional literature. We refer, of course, to the capacity that is unique to Homo sapiens—indoctrinabilty. As we argue in chapter 7, it is this remarkable human trait that, despite our species' natural hierarchical inclinations, sometimes makes a viable democracy possible.

At this point, though, it is essential to look first at the aforementioned and more commonly recognized enabling or prerequisite material conditions. Since there is a near consensus that it is the internal conditions that are the more important, we will start with these.

One more preliminary comment: Although the distinction is not always explicit in the literature, we should distinguish between those factors that are seen as critical in the *emergence* of a democracy and those that are viewed as significantly contributing to the *continuation* of democratic governance. Since we will deal with the latter in some detail in our concluding chapter, we will here focus on the former.

INTERNAL PREREQUISITES

Among the internal conditions that have been most often associated with the birth of democracy are a reasonably equitable distribution of wealth; a comparatively high level of education; urbanization; effective communication networks; ethnic, linguistic and religious unity; the presence of a dissatisfied "out elite"; the competence and flexibility of the existing regime; prior experience with democratic institutions; and a supportive political culture. We will look briefly at each of these.

Distribution of Wealth

Almost 2,500 years ago, Aristotle discerned a relationship between the distribution of wealth and the likelihood of democracy. The lesser the inequalities of the former, he postulated, the greater the chances for the latter. Gibbon, in company with almost all subsequent historians, pointed to the vast disparities between the wealthy and the increasingly impoverished masses as one of the major factors leading to the decline and ultimate fall of the republic (and of democracy) in Rome. And during his visit to the United States, de Tocqueville was struck "by the general equality of condition among the people" (1963, bk. 1, p. 3). That equality, he was convinced, contributed greatly to the American brand of democracy.[2]

Supporting this contention, more recent, systematic, and statistically oriented studies indicate that greater income equality within a country is associated with greater odds of democracy occurring therein (Muller, 1988; Muller and Seligson, 1994). Furthermore, according to Vanhanen (1984), widespread and relatively even land ownership is another consistent corre- late of democracy. And of course there have been many studies of the relationship between economic crises and the breakdown of democratic governance.[3]

Turning to a somewhat more exotic measure, energy consumption is highly correlated with wealth per capita and is considered by some to be a reliable measure of national economic well-being (Burkhart and Lewis- Beck, 1994).[4] Energy consumption per person, in turn, is associated with degree of democratization (Burkhart and Lewis-Beck, 1994). In short, greater national wealth per capita and lower levels of income inequality (and of land ownership) appear to provide a markedly more nurturing environ- ment for the development of democracy.

Education

Democracy demands a great deal of its people. If democracies are to evolve and survive, their citizens must be able to understand the issues of the day, be willing to engage in political activities, and, *de minimis*, cast ballots that have some logical relationship to these issues and to the direction in which they wish their country to move. Furthermore, and no small matter, they should have a basic sense of the political as well as the legal and moral importance of protecting minority rights.

In theory, education should contribute significantly to the ability of a citizenry to satisfy these demands; in practice, this actually seems to be the case, if perhaps not to the full degree that one might hope (Page and Shapiro, 1992). A number of studies have shown that more literate populations and higher levels of education, in terms of average number of years of schooling and higher proportions of people going on to college, are all associated with a greater likelihood of democratic governance (Deutsch, 1961; McCrone and Cnudde, 1967; Banks, 1972; Vanhanen, 1984).

Urbanization

One of the most commonly encountered conclusions is that urbanization facilitates the emergence of democracy. The underlying idea seems to be that agricultural societies are more traditional and thus more accepting of authoritarian polities (Lerner, 1958). Urbanization, however, usually brings with it greater wealth, more widespread education, and (see later discussion) denser communication networks. The end result, presumably, is that more highly urbanized nations have a greater receptivity to change and to nontraditional modes of behavior, and thus a relatively greater possibility of becoming democracies (Cutright, 1963; McCrone and Cnudde, 1967; Banks, 1972; Vanhanen, 1984).

Perhaps. But this criterion is hardly unambiguous. Is urbanization to be ascertained by the existence of sizable cities; by the percentage of the population living, respectively, in the city and in the countryside; or by some measure of population density? Besides, there have been many nations that have had huge urban populations (Babylonia, Assyria, Egypt, Persia, Imperial Rome, etc.) or today have great cities (China and Russia are the most obvious examples) where the purported relationship between urbanization and democracy has yet to be perceived. Or, to come at the matter from another direction, did urbanization really play a significant role in the development of democracy in, say, Switzerland, England, and the United States?[5] Of all the putative requisites, this may be one of the most arguable.

Communication Networks

At the time of the Tiananmen Square confrontation in China, many commentators insisted that modern communication systems, as exemplified by radio, television, fax machines and E-mail, doomed the incumbent communist regime. Maybe or maybe not; the jury is still out on that prediction.[6] A plausible case has been made, though, that denser communication networks enhance the probability of democracy emerging and flourishing (Deutsch, 1961). Indeed, considerable evidence has since accumulated that such networks are associated with democratization (Cutright, 1963; Lipset, 1963; McCrone and Cnudde, 1967; Neubauer, 1967; Banks, 1972).

The idea does have a certain intuitive appeal. Presumably, better communications lead to more and better information; better information, it would seem, enhances the ability of the citizenry to take part in a democratic dialogue and, again presumably, to vote knowledgeably on the issues of the day.

Ethnic, Linguistic, and Religious Unity

On a priori grounds, we might expect that democracy would have a more difficult time taking root in societies that are multiethnic and/or multilinguistic or those in which there are profound religious cleavages. Problems of ready communication aside, conflicts and misunderstandings among different groups with different ethnic backgrounds, languages, and religious beliefs would tend to militate against the development of a commonly accepted democratic civic culture.

All too often, we know, these differences go hand in hand with age-old suspicions and animosities. These are sometimes so deep-seated, and the understanding of past events is sometimes so radically at variance, that the constituent populations have totally different conceptions of past events— and inhabit what seem to be fundamentally dissimilar if not inherently incompatible worlds. Nor are people who do not share common under- standings and who profoundly distrust each other likely to be overly con- cerned about the civil and political rights of those whom they regard as their historical enemies.

Not surprisingly, there is considerable evidence that democracy is much less likely to take root in countries characterized by this type of cultural fragmentation (Muller and Seligson, 1994). For example, the "old" Soviet Union, and in many instances the individual republics as well, were multi- ethnic societies held together in large part by totalitarian methods. With the disintegration of the central government and the subsequent peeling away of a host of newly sovereign states, these ethnic, linguistic, and religious differences, with their long-held legacy of grievances and hatreds, have been an important factor militating against the creation of democratic govern- ment. The "ethnic cleansing" that took place in what was formerly Yugosla- via provides an even clearer, and far more horrendous, instance of what can occur among such culturally heterogeneous populations.

Still, on this matter, the historical record is somewhat mixed. Thus, in both the Athenian and Roman democracies, the citizens shared a common language and a common religion. This was also the situation in England and the United States where, despite the existence of a Catholic minority, the majority and dominant religion was Protestant in the latter and Episcopalian in the former—and English, until quite recently, was the overwhelmingly predominant tongue.

On the other hand, the Swiss democracy took root among a population that was both multilingual and religiously diverse; much the same was true in Canada. The Dutch shared, for the most part, a common language but were (and of course still are) divided religiously; in Belgium there were both religious and linguistic cleavages. Yet both countries evolved highly viable democratic governments. And, to introduce another obvi- ous reservation, there are many countries that have an overwhelmingly dominant religion, a nigh universal language—and a resolutely authori- tarian political system.

A Disaffected "Out Elite"

In human history, the normal mode of governance is, of course, authoritarian, or, as civilization flowered in the twentieth century, totalitarian. This is the normal mode in two senses: first, it is by far the most common type of polity encountered wherever the state has emerged; second, to repeat our basic thesis, it is the type of political order to which we have been predisposed by our evolutionary history.

For a democracy to emerge in the face of this inherent contradisposition, the scholarly consensus holds, some combination of the above material enabling conditions is required. Also required, to cite a somewhat older body of thought, is a disaffected "out elite."[7]

By this term we mean an influential, though not necessarily large, group of individuals who, though possessing some substantial combination of education, wealth, and status, feel that their interests are not being satisfactorily furthered by the existent political system. A classic example of such an out elite, almost needless to say, is a rising middle class in a state whose political machinery is controlled and whose political decisions are being made by a powerful monarch, a hereditary aristocracy, and/or a landed plutocracy.[8]

In such a situation, the natural first desire of the out elite is to secure admission to, and an effective voice in, the existent political establishment. Where these ruling classes are sufficiently sagacious, as Pareto and Mosca have emphasized, they provide an adequate opportunity for that entry. The resulting "circulation of elites" lends itself both to political stability and the perpetuation of the existing system. Where the ruling classes lack this political foresight, those who feel that they are politically disenfranchised are left with no alternative but to demand that the existing system itself be changed.

Since that system is almost always authoritarian in nature, the out elite tactically have few options but to become the advocates of, and spokesmen for, a more democratic order. Toward that end, consequently, they adopt a political rhetoric in which the concepts of enlarged representation, civil liberties, and even political equality are increasingly salient, even though their own political preferences and desires may fall considerably short of what we would today regard as a truly democratic polity.

If the out elite are effective propagandists, and especially where the existing system is, or is perceived as being, unduly unfair, harsh, or exploitative, the unique human capacity that we have called "indoctrinability" (see chapter 7) may make it possible for them to win over to "democracy" a politically significant segment of the population. When this ideological

accomplishment coincides with some combination of the requisites mentioned, then—and perhaps only then—does there exist a full complement
of the conditions essential for the emergence, or more precisely, at least the
beginnings, of a democratic polity.

Wisdom and Flexibility of the Existent Regime

As just suggested, but not always singled out for explicit mention, the
political intelligence and adaptability of the "in elite" is another important
element in the equation. Granting that their actions were not always purely
voluntary, the English monarchs (and their political supporters) gave way,
step by step, during the late eighteenth and early nineteenth centuries,
making possible the peaceful, gradual emergence of democracy in England.

For a striking contrast, we need only reflect on the ultimately fatal policy
of the Bourbons. What might have been the history of France, of Europe,
and possibly of the world itself, had Louis XVI and his advisors been more
politically astute? In one ironic respect, though, they were quite successful:
their obduracy set into motion forces that were to delay the emergence of
democracy in France for almost another century.

The Bourbons, though, had no monopoly on stubbornness and inflexibil-
ity. Learning either too little or too much from the French Revolution,
European monarchical regimes, from Waterloo until the middle of the
nineteenth century, did their best to suppress nascent democratic movements. Over the short run, they were quite successful. As a consequence,
political revolution rather than evolution was the midwife of the democracies born in 1848—and their traumatic birth undoubtedly was an important
factor in their subsequent uncertain, unhealthy, and all too often quite brief
existence.[9] Romanov Russia provides a classic example of how long, and
how effectively, a determinedly blind regime can stultify even very modest
proposals for democratic change[10]—and of what destructive forces can be
unleashed when that policy ultimately fails.[11]

Prior History as Democracies

Recent history suggests, first, that democracy has a better chance of
survival in the small handful of countries that have had some previous
experience with that form of government. That is, in countries that were
once democratic, subsequently became authoritarian, and, again changing,
once again attempt democratic governance. The experience of Germany and
what was previously called Czechoslovakia, both of which had a few

decades of democratic governance before falling upon totalitarian times, would seem to justify that conclusion.

History also seems to suggest, second, that countries with a continuing tradition of democracy are more likely to *remain* democratic. There is some evidence that both years of continuous democracy and the historical level of democracy (from partial democracy to strong democracy) affect how democratic a nation is at any given point in time (Muller and Seligson, 1994).

On the other hand, prior—and famously impressive—life as a democracy did not seem measurably to hasten or assist its rebirth in either Greece or Italy, where some twenty centuries elapsed between the demise and the reemergence of that mode of governance.[12]

Predisposing Civic Culture

"Political culture" refers to the set of values and beliefs that are held by any given polity. A democratic civic culture is characterized, of course, by a (relative) tolerance for opposing opinions, belief in voting as a way of selecting leaders and setting policy, and acceptance of competing political parties and candidates as appropriate vehicles for organizing electoral choices. There is also some evidence indicating that such attitudes as life satisfaction, interpersonal trust, and lack of support for radical change enhance democratic functioning (Inglehart, 1990; Putnam, Leonardi, and Nanetti, 1993),[13] although the existence of such a relationship has been questioned (Muller and Seligson, 1994).

A striking feature of the American civic culture, de Tocqueville wrote in 1840, was that "Americans of all ages, all conditions, and all dispositions constantly form associations" (1945, bk. 1:198). And according to a recent (Dec. 23, 1995:29–30) *Economist* essay entitled "America's Strange Clubs," that is still our practice (although, disturbingly enough, this civic involvement may be decreasing. See Putnam, 1995a, 1995b).

Even in authoritarian states, these associational activities can serve as condensation points for a shadow democratic culture out of which a functioning democracy might subsequently emerge. Vaclav Havel (1990) and Adam Michnik (1986) have written touchingly of the gradual development, in Czechoslovakia, of a more democratic civic culture, via a process of small, painful incremental steps.

It began with petitions signed by leading figures in the art world—exemplified by groups such as Charter 77—protesting the jailing of some individual or another for alleged "anti-state" machinations. At first, the signatories were themselves threatened with, or actually subjected to, imprisonment. But as time went on and the pressure from "below" increased, the government slowly came to allow more openness. In the process, as Havel puts it, "people's civic backbones began to straighten out again" (1990:182). By taking action, the Czechs began to live as if there were greater freedom than actually existed; they began to practice freedom and democratic involvement. Consequently, when the Soviet chains were finally loosed, there were already in existence the basic elements of a democratic civic culture.

The Czechs had, to be sure, a democratic past on which to draw—and they had, in Havel, Michnik, and their associates, some extraordinarily insightful democratic figures. Admittedly, the situation there was atypical. However, the task of creating a favorable civic culture is one that faces all aspiring democratic movements, and there may be much to be learned from the tactics developed by the Czechoslovakian democratic leadership.

We should keep in mind, though, that we are speaking of the internal requisites of democracy. Where democracy has, in effect, been imposed from the outside, as it was for contemporary Japan, even the rudiments of a democratic civic culture may be essentially absent. The implications of that absence for the long-term prospects of democratic government in Japan remain to be seen. As we remark in the next chapter, after fifty years the Japanese have yet to experience a substantively meaningful transfer of power from one elected party to another.

Do Nine Internal Prerequisites Yield an Algorithm?

Is it possible to give each of these nine "internal" prerequisites (or any others which come to mind) a numerical value or, failing that, to resolve how many of them, or which of them and to what degree, must be present to give rise to a viable democratic government? With all respect to the many distinguished scholars who have wrestled with this problem, we think that the answer, pending further substantial advances in the social sciences, is still no.

We say this for several reasons. To begin, and to repeat a now familiar refrain, the "set" of democracies still remains too small—and in some instances too new—to permit much more than broad generalizations, almost all subject to many exceptions. Furthermore, several of the best examples and longest lived of such governments (i.e., the United States, Canada, Australia)[14] are "democracies by descent" in that many of their postindependence political institutions and practices were modeled after, or inherited from, their common parent. And, as noted above and again later, an analogous external influence was certainly the determinative factor in launching today's democratic Japan.

In addition, some of the aforementioned internal prerequisites are quite difficult to measure. This is true in two senses: first (as with ethnic, linguistic, and religious unity or a predisposing civic culture), it is difficult to determine whether they actually exist; and second, even where we can agree that they are present, it is hard to know whether they approach the presumably essential critical level (education, communication networks, broad equality of wealth, and urbanization come to mind). Lacking the ability satisfactorily to measure these factors, their presence or absence is thus often a matter of subjective judgement.

Another complicating element in the equation must also be recognized. The critical combination of internal and, as we will see, external factors may well vary considerably from one era to another. Conceivably, certain combinations might suffice when a nation is in a preindustrial condition, other combinations may be needed for industrialized countries, and yet a third mix might be in order where, in currently fashionable terminology, a postindustrialized society is attempting the transition to democracy.

Given these limitations and constraints, it is difficult to escape the conclusion that we do not as yet have a satisfactory understanding of the precise constellation of internal conditions whose existence makes democracy sometimes possible—and whose absence, other factors being constant—probably dooms the effort to failure.

EXTERNAL REQUISITE CONDITIONS

Conditions external to a given country, as in the case of post–World War II Japan, can also have a direct bearing upon its chances for democratization (Sorenson, 1993). Among these are colonial status, regional factors, and the possible interest of competing powers.

Colonial Status: Mother Country Policies

As we have seen, the likelihood of postindependence democratic governance is much greater in those nations formerly governed by nations that were themselves democratic and permitted, if they did not actually encourage, the development of democratic political institutions in their former colonies. England (or Great Britain) is the classic exemplar: Many of its former possessions became democracies whether they achieved their freedom via revolution, as in the case of the United States, or in more peaceful fashion, à la Canada and Australia. Still, although a colonial power may deliberately labor to leave such a legacy, there is no assurance that it will be successful, as demonstrated by the discouraging political developments in Uganda, Kenya, Nigeria, and, until quite recently, South Africa.

In this respect, England (or Great Britain) stood almost alone. Among colonial subjects, democratic and separatist (i.e., those seeking independence) movements tend to go hand in hand (see chapter 8). Not surprisingly, most imperial nations try to discourage, if not actively repress, both tendencies among their colonies. This was certainly the policy followed by France, Spain, Portugal, Germany, Belgium, Holland, and, after the turn of the twentieth-century, Japan.

From a long-term perspective, the policy seems to have been more successful than expected—or desired. It is hardly coincidental, to borrow a phrase badly tarnished by its Marxist associations, that almost every one of these nations' former colonies, from Algeria to Zambia, adopted—or evolved—some type of authoritarian, if not totalitarian, government after it achieved independence.

Regional Factors

The history of Eastern Europe after World War II provides abundant evidence that democracy has a dismal life expectancy where the region is dominated by an overwhelmingly powerful state. Under Stalin and his successors in the USSR, nascent democratic tendencies were brutally repressed in Hungary and Czechoslovakia and bitterly, if ultimately unsuccessfully, opposed when they manifested themselves in Poland. Nor did the malign consequences end with the dissolution of the Soviet empire. Contrary to what many optimistically expected, and what some still persist in believing, most of the governments of the liberated former satellite Soviet states, as well as that of Russia itself, have been authoritarian, rather than democratic, in nature.

There was nothing novel, to be sure, in the spectacle of a regionally dominant power consciously seeking to stamp out even embryonic democratic (and nationalistic) movements in that part of the world over which it claims hegemony. This was the policy followed with considerable success by Austria-Hungary until World War I and, a century or two earlier, by Spain in the Netherlands and elsewhere.

Superpower Rivalry

Another external factor bearing on the prospects of successful democracy in a given country is the extent to which such success (or failure) coincides with the interests of a superpower[15] when that power is engaged in a struggle for supremacy with another political titan. Normally, we could expect a given superpower to give aid and assistance to those nations whose governmental system and ideology coincided with its own, especially when that contest occurred in a geographic area both powers deemed important. This ideological (and geopolitical) fit was nicely demonstrated during the cold war by the abundant moral, military, and financial assistance that Israel received from the United States and by the opposing Soviet policy of generally supporting Israel's Arab enemies.

Matters, though, do not always work out so neatly. As an unknown genius once remarked, "politics makes strange bedfellows," an aphorism as true in foreign as it is in domestic policy. The United States, for instance, regularly gave aid and comfort—sometimes intervening directly and not too covertly—to authoritarian regimes in Latin America and elsewhere, when these regimes were challenged by an opposition that often seemed to seek, it seems fair to say, a more democratic mode of government (Schoultz, Smith, and Varos, 1994). The official rationale, it will be recalled, was that these movements (such as the Sandanistas, to take a well-known instance), were really communist inspired and that their victory would work to the advantage of the USSR. In other words, government apologists argued, democracy was actually being furthered by our support of what were in truth de facto dictatorships. This policy, some have insisted, was not limited to Latin America, then or now, nor is it one on which the United States has a monopoly. In international rivalries, we have repeatedly seen, ideology frequently takes a back seat to power politics.

Global Fashion

Democracies, Huntington has written (1991, 1991–1992), tend to be launched in periodic waves. The existence of such a tidal movement may therefore be a factor in whether a given nation opts to adopt that form of government. Rustow puts it somewhat differently, suggesting that democratic "role models" inspire other countries to move in that direction. He may be right, although recent events suggest that he is overly sanguine in deriving from this tendency the conclusion "that the world, in what promises to be more than a half-century of peace, has become safer for democracy than it was in 1945, 1917, or at any previous time" (1980:91). Rustow's confidence notwithstanding, it remains to be demonstrated that the few democracies that have come into existence during the past decade or two will, given our species' behavioral bias, be able to demonstrate any greater longevity than those born after World War I.[16]

CONCLUDING COMMENT

As social primates, we have been endowed by natural selection with a predilection for hierarchical social and political structures. With fairly few exceptions, consequently, Homo sapiens' typical polity tends to be hierarchical and authoritarian in form and function. Still, though this is by far the most commonly encountered mode of government, democracies occasionally emerge, and some even survive for a fairly substantial time. How does this happen?

Drawing on the established literature, we have identified nine internal prerequisite or enabling conditions. While scholars generally agree upon these fundamental requirements, there is as yet no consensus as to precisely what combination is needed for an authoritarian regime to transform itself into a democracy.

There are, in addition, at least four external factors that, in some combination with the nine internal requirements, may either facilitate or make near impossible the successful emergence of democracy in a given polity or polities. Here again, we can only speculate upon the relative importance of these factors and the manner in which, interacting with some combination of internal enabling conditions, they may shape or even have a determinative influence on the final outcome.

On one aspect of this issue, though, we can speak with greater assurance. Whatever the relative importance of the internal and external factors—and that importance may well vary considerably from situation to situation—both are only necessary rather than sufficient conditions for the birth and continuing survival of a democratic government. One more factor, also a necessary but probably not a sufficient condition, is essential. We refer, of course, to that uniquely human attribute, indoctrinability. Not to vex the reader but simply out of organizational necessity, we have postponed further discussion of the rare enabling trait to part 3, which deals with that topic, as well as the other relevant social and political proclivities with which natural selection has so generously endowed our species.

NOTES

1. Ideally, this would be exemplified by at least one peaceful change of ruling party within, say, the past 20 or so years.

2. "The whole country," he observed, "seems to have melded into one middle class" (1945, bk. 1, p. 53).

3. See, for example, O'Donnell (1973), Linz (1978). For an excellent summary of the recent literature, see Gasiorowski (1995).

4. Whether—or how—this is applicable to preindustrial democracies such as Athens and Rome is manifestly unclear.

5. Thomas Jefferson, in fact, saw the aggregation of population in cities as a major threat to democracy.

6. As events have made all too clear, the collapse of communism by no means ensures or automatically leads to a democratic polity or polities.

7. Mosca (1939) and Pareto (1935); more recently, see Lasswell and Leites (1949).

8. About 2 months after this sentence was originally written, *The Wall Street Journal* ran a report entitled "A Rising Middle Class Clamors for Changes in Troubled Pakistan." One of the sentences in the report read, "A fast-swelling population and nascent middle class are clamoring for a wider stake in a system dominated by a landowner and business oligarchy that pays almost no taxes yet holds most power" (December 14, 1995, p. 1).

9. "It is commonly [at] the outset of a democratic society," wrote de Tocqueville, "that citizens are most disposed to live apart. . . . Those members of the community who were at the top . . . cannot forget their former greatness [while those] who were formerly at the foot of the social scale . . . cannot enjoy their newly acquired independence without secret uneasiness" (quoted in *The Economist*, Nov. 25, 1995, p. 15).

10. Czarist Russian history is replete, we cannot forbear to add, with examples of the innate human tendency to obey, a tendency discussed at some length in chapter 6.

11. That failure, historians generally agree, was greatly accelerated by the defeat of the Russian armies in World War I. How long Czarist absolutism would have otherwise endured, absent the equivalent of a Romanov Gorbachev, we can only speculate.

12. As we note in chapter 4, there may be some question as to whether Greece satisfies even our "soft" definition of democracy.

13. For a critique of Putnam's work, see Tarrow (1996).

14. And to the extent that they warrant this classification (see chapter 4), India and South Africa as well.

15. Or to use a more recent terminology, a "core state" (Wallerstein, 1974; Burkhart and Lewis-Beck, 1994).

16. The underlying contention here seems to be that democracies tend to beget democracies. Also, democracies appear to fight other democracies less. To the extent, then, that war can threaten democracy, the more democracies there are, the less threat to a country's existence as a democracy (see Merritt and Zinnes, 1991; Russett and Antholis, 1992; Maoz and Russett, 1993; Russett, 1993). At least an equally persuasive case can be made, we think, that totalitarian states beget totalitarian states, as happened after World War I and again, in Eastern and Central Europe, after World War II.

Chapter 4

Will the Real Democracies
Please Stand Up

SETTING THE PROBLEM

Given our contention that evolution has inclined our species to favor authoritarian and hierarchical political systems, we must be prepared to adduce two types of supporting evidence. First, that Homo sapiens share the tendencies toward dominance relations, hierarchy, and obedience that characterize all the other social primates. Ample, and we trust persuasive, documentation of these familial traits will be provided later in part 3, "The Neo-Darwinian Case and Supporting Evidence."

Second, our argument also demands supporting evidence for the claim that, given our innate authoritarian tendencies, (1) democracies have been rare in the past, and (2) despite what is widely hailed as the Age of Democracy, they still remain very much a minority mode of governance. Since there can be little doubt about the rarity of democratic governments in past centuries, our assertion (or "prediction") of their continued infrequency today, even after the collapse of Soviet-bloc totalitarianism, thus becomes an acid test of our thesis.

In that sense, this is a pivotal chapter. If democracies are now the predominant form of government, that would certainly cast doubt on our neo-Darwinian explanation of why they have been so infrequent in past centuries. If, however, democracies still remain a minority among polities, that persistent phenomenon is consistent with and, we think it fair to say, gives further credence to an explanation that treats our evolutionary history as a major contributing factor.

In conducting our census of democratic states, we have divided political history into three periods: (1) from classical times to circa 1850, (2) from 1850 to 1990, and (3) the contemporary world, that is, from 1990 to 1995. We use 1850 as one of the key dates because by then the United States had clearly emerged as a democratic country, and we can then trace the gradual appearance of other democracies over the next near century and a half.

Before attempting any tally, though, we need a satisfactory working definition that will enable us to separate the democratic sheep from the nondemocratic goats. That, then, becomes our initial task.

DEMOCRACY: THE BASIC CHARACTERISTICS

Following a hallowed if not especially imaginative tradition, we turned initially to a political dictionary.[1] The definition offered there declares that democracy is

a system of government in which ultimate political authority is vested in the people. . . . Democracy may be direct, as practiced in ancient Athens and in New England town meetings, or indirect and representative. . . . Democracy requires a decision-making system based on majority rule, with minority rights protected.

This definition pretty well captures the two basic essentials of a democracy upon which practically all scholars agree.[2] Succinctly put, these are (1) government by the majority, and (2) what is usually called "the rule of law."[3] A brief comment on each of these is undoubtedly in order.

Majority Rule

Practically everyone who has written on the subject includes under majority rule a representative system of government, freely contested and meaningful elections, ultimate accountability of the representatives to the electorate, and equal weight of voting influence in the sense of wide, if not universal, suffrage embodying the principle, "one person, one vote." (We limit our discussion here to representative democracy since this has been the form of all democracies at the national level since Athenian days.)

In a democratic system, the representatives are chosen by some type of popular vote, the specific method varying considerably from one country to another. To be truly democratic, the system must enable the majority—if there is a majority—to elect a roughly corresponding proportion of the representatives. Ideally, though not always invariably, the same provision would be made for some equitable method of minority representation. In all democracies, representatives are responsible to the electorate in that they are chosen by their constituents[4] and reelection is contingent upon the voters of that constituency.

Meaningful and openly contested elections demand some type of bi- or multiparty competition and the ability of all parties to put their case before the electorate to the best of the resources available to them. Elections may be openly contested, but if one party is completely dominant, it need pay little attention to what the people desire, since there is no meaningful alternative to which the voter can turn (Key, 1949). Where a single party remains in office election after election, as has been the case in Latin America and elsewhere, there may be a legitimate question as to whether this criterion is being satisfied. Our own feeling is that "meaningful elections" should entail at least one major peaceful (i.e., electoral) turnover of office over, say, a 20-year span.

Majority rule also calls for a suffrage that gives the vote to most of the adult citizenry. Even those countries invariably recognized as democracies sometimes fall considerably short of universal suffrage because age, residence, literacy (and in one well-publicized instance, sex) qualifications may deny the ballot to some, or possibly a significant fraction, of the population.

The Rule of Law

All of the aforementioned requirements, as well as a long list of civil rights and liberties, may be spelled out in a nation's constitution and laws. Nonetheless, as we have too often seen, these are of little value absent a judicial system capable of their effective enforcement. That, in essence, is what is meant by the term "the rule of law."

Electoral rights and civil liberties need to be more than fine words on exquisite parchment. If those who lose an election are stripped of their civil rights, freedom, or property by a victorious majority, that is a dubious form of democracy. The rule of law requires an independent judiciary, a government willing to enforce even those judicial decisions it dislikes, and the effective protection of political and civil liberties against both public and private infringement. The American institution of an independent judiciary still remains the basic model in this respect and may well constitute the single most important American contribution to democratic theory and practice.

Majority rule and the rule of law are thus the two indispensable components of democratic governance. The great irony, of course, is that while both are absolutely essential, they often conflict with each other and, as a result, have been a source of ongoing political controversy. But this fundamental contradiction simply cannot be escaped: it is the price of living in a democracy.

A concluding comment on majority rule and the rule of law: Admittedly, neither of these two requirements lends itself to very satisfactory quantification; in some instances opinions about a given country will legitimately differ. Still, when we look at the several assessments and listings of democratic and nondemocratic governments cited, there is far more agreement than disagreement. To paraphrase Justice Potter Stewart's famous comment about pornography, we may not be able precisely to define a democracy— but we usually know one when we see one.

HISTORICAL EMERGENCE OF DEMOCRATIC GOVERNMENTS

From Athenian Times to 1850

Very few will challenge the proposition that until the first half of the nineteenth century, Athens and then Rome constitute the total set of democratic polities. Athens may not have quite satisfied the "rule of law" requirement but, on the other hand, the Athenians had a truly remarkable

faith in the potential and actual wisdom of mass audiences. Rather than deferring to elite expertise when it came time to make important decisions, the citizenry believed itself to be collectively the best possible judge of important matters. (Ober, 1993:484)[5]

As the condemnation of Socrates vividly illustrates, the almost inevitable clash between the will of the majority and what we would regard as the legitimate exercise of civil freedoms was usually resolved in favor of the former.

The Roman Republic provided a much better democratic exemplar for later ages. Under the Republic, and probably until the emperors were accepted as near deities, the will of the majority and the actions of governmental officials were seen as properly constrained by Roman law.

Possibly because of this, Roman democracy was the longer lived of the two, although Athens's defeat by Sparta almost certainly hastened, if it did not actually cause, the demise of popular rule. In any event, majority governance in Athens lasted considerably less than a century by the most generous reckoning. The much longer lived Roman democracy, on the other hand, was destroyed from within.

With the collapse of the Roman Republic, democracy disappeared from the world scene as a form of national government.[6] The resulting nearly 2,000-year hiatus was finally broken in the midnineteenth century by the United States, which, it is generally agreed, was the first of the modern democratic polities. There is, to be sure, some question as to the exact point at which the American republic actually merited this designation. Some would date it from the election of 1828, some a bit earlier, others a bit later. Beyond dispute, though, by 1850 democracy had once again made an appearance, albeit numerically a most modest appearance, in the family of nations.

From 1850 to 1990

Considering the substantial time span involved and the many changes that occurred over the next century and a half, we thought it best to provide a decade-by-decade running account rather than a simple "beginning and end of era" tabulation. For this reason, we will start with, and borrow liberally from, Tatu Vanhanen (1990), who has conducted this type of analysis.

We must emphasize, however, that Vanhanen relies entirely on two voting statistics[7] and simply ignores the presence or absence of what we have called the "rule of law." Consequently, he sometimes awards the accolade to countries where other students, applying both criteria, would firmly deny it. This will become quite apparent when we later turn to Robert Dahl, who has utilized more stringent standards and whose political barometer, when the two assessments diverge, yields more defensible results.

According to Vanhanen (1990), modern democracies emerged in the following order:

1. 1850–1859. Only one, the United States.
2. 1860–1869. Canada joins the United States.
3. 1870–1879. The United States, Canada, and France.
4. 1880–1889. Switzerland enters the club.
5. 1890–1899. Belgium and New Zealand are added. At the turn of the century, then, 6 (or 14 percent) of the 43 countries in Vanhanen's count are democracies.
6. 1900–1909. Australia, Norway, and Holland pass muster.
7. 1910–1919. Several newcomers—Denmark, Finland, the United Kingdom, and Sweden. Of 51 countries, 14 (27 percent) are now democratic.

8. 1920–1929. Eleven new countries are formed during this decade. Vanhanen classifies Ireland, Poland, Czechoslovakia, Yugoslavia, Uruguay, Germany, and Costa Rica as democratic. Italy, under Mussolini, drops out. According to Vanhanen, 21 of 62 countries (34 percent) are democracies.

9. 1930–1939. A decade of great political turmoil. Spain, very briefly, is the lone new entrant to the democratic set. Of 63 countries, 20 (or 19 if Spain is deleted) are democracies. This is the period when, according to Huntington, the "first wave" of democratic governments begins to recede (1991, 1991–1992).

10. 1940–1949. The new democracies listed are Sri Lanka, Cuba, Japan, Israel, the Philippines, Lebanon, and Hungary (very briefly). We forebear to comment on Vanhanen's generosity, which brings the percentage of democracies (26 of 74 nations) to 33 percent.

11. 1950–1959. Now recognized as democracies are Brazil, Turkey, India, Chile, Burma, South Korea, Panama, and Argentina. Again, no comment. Vanhanen's incidence of democracies reaches 39 percent.

12. 1960–1969. There are now 117 states, of which, Vanhanen says, Lesotho, Guyana, Venezuela, Trinidad and Tobago, Jamaica, Malaysia, Sierra Leone, and Somalia, are to be regarded as democracies. Once again, though with difficulty, no comment.

13. 1970–1979. Argentina, the Philippines, and South Korea drop from the democratic roster; Colombia, El Salvador, and Fiji are added. The ratio of democracies (36 of 119 countries) declines to 30 percent, consistent with Huntington's concept of a second wave.

14. 1980–1989. The number of countries rises to 147, and of democracies to 61 (or 41 percent), by Vanhanen's count.

As mentioned above, Vanhanen's assessments frequently vary from those of Robert Dahl (1971, 1991), who defines democracy somewhat differently and, in our judgment, more appropriately. For example, Dahl's minimum requirements for democracy include freedom to form and join organizations, freedom of expression, the right to vote, eligibility for public office, the right of, political leaders to compete for support, alternative sources of information, free and fair elections, and institutions for making governmental policies that depend on votes and other expressions of popular preference (1971:3).

Dahl uses several sources to trace the increase in the number of both polyarchies (a term the functional equivalent of democracy) and nonpolyarchies from 1850 through 1989. Like Vanhanen (who happens to be one of his sources), Dahl reports an increase in the number of polyarchies over time. More interesting, though, is that while the number of polyarchies closed the gap on nonpolyarchies a couple of times historically (in the decades of the 1920s and 1950s, for example), the gap has widened in the last three decades. And never has a majority of countries been polyarchies, according to Dahl.

Figure 1, which gives the percentage of democratic governments as compared to the total number of governments at any point in time, is more directly relevant to our inquiry. Here we see that the proportion of countries classified as democratic peaked in the 1950s, then declined during the ensuing three decades.

Vanhanen's reliance on voting data led him, as the examples given testify, to overestimate substantially both the number and thus the percentage of democracies in the constellation of national states during this roughly 150-year span. But even by his extraordinarily charitable count, democratic governments were always in a definite minority; even his high-water mark, it will be recalled, reached only 41 percent (for the 1980–1989 decade). A more demanding assessment, applying Dahl's criteria, reduces that percentage very sharply, as Figure 1 demonstrates.

Figure 1
Percentage of Polyarchies

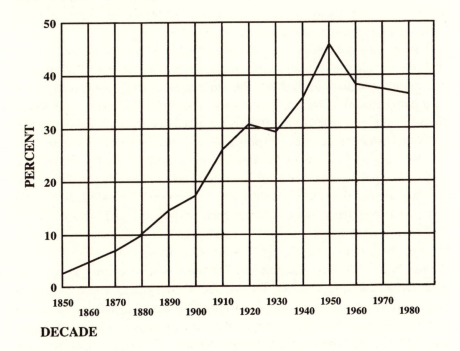

Source: Dahl (1991:77)

DEMOCRACY IN THE WORLD TODAY

How many democracies are there in the world today? The first step is to weed out the manifest noncandidates and arrive at a manageable short list. Toward that end, we draw on the findings of six recent studies. These are:

1. Vanhanen's aforementioned enumeration as of 1988

2. Dahl's polyarchy project listing as of 1985 (Coppedge and Reinicke, 1991)

3. McColm's 1991 Freedom House survey (McColm, 1991)

4. Gastil's ranking of democracies (Gastil, 1991)

5. Bollen's rating of countries as of 1980 (Bollen, 1993)

6. Sullivan's evaluations as of 1992 (Sullivan, 1992)

These six were selected because they employ a variety of metrics to assay how democratic a given nation is considered to be. While they differ slightly in approach and terminology, somewhat complicating exact comparisons, almost all use the majority rule and rule of law criteria, and their findings, Vanhanen aside, are consistent with one another.

That is, they are consistent with each other in all but one respect. Some analysts include microstates (customarily defined as nations with less than one million population) such as Fiji, Dominica, Grenada, and so forth, in their compilations; some analysts do not. The obvious solution here was to simply exclude the microstates from our count. For one thing, some of them[8] are little better than colonies, and their existence as sovereign states frequently more de jure than de facto. More to the point, though, they encompass so few people that they really confound rather than enlighten analysis.

We made our first cut by identifying "consensus" democracies. We did this by counting the number of times each country is listed (among the six studies) as a democracy, and then by singling out those that are so identified three or more times. Plainly, those most often ranked as democratic were the best bets for further examination. The process was not quite as straightforward as it seems, however, for our six studies sweep across a 12-year period. Consequently, countries that might have been labeled democratic at one point in time but later changed their mode of governance got fewer "points." This built into our tabulation a modest requirement of democratic stability.

The "Consensus" Democracies: The Initial Short List

The macrocountries surviving the first cut, that is, those that received three or more identifications as democracies from our six studies are, in alphabetical order:

Argentina	Italy
Australia	Jamaica
Austria	Japan
Belgium	Mauritius
Bolivia	Netherlands
Botswana	New Zealand
Brazil	Norway
Canada	Papua (New Guinea)
Colombia	Peru
Costa Rica	Philippines
Denmark	Portugal
Dominican Republic	South Korea
Ecuador	Spain
Finland	Sweden
France	Switzerland
Germany	Trinidad and Tobago
Greece	United Kingdom
Honduras	United States
India	Uruguay
Ireland	Venezuela
Israel	

With a short list in hand, our next step was to look at it in light of recent events, utilizing such current sources as *The New York Times*, *The Economist*, and Freedom House's regular surveys as a further check (we used the listings for rating countries in 1993, published in *The Economist* (August 27, 1994:16), and in 1995 [Karatnycky, 1996]). The task here, almost needless to say, was to determine whether political developments in very recent years may have ended democracy in some of these countries—or brought it about in others. So considered, legitimate questions can be raised about quite a few governments on this initial roster. Examples follow:

Latin America

The Dominican Republic's President Belaguer was recently elected to his sixth consecutive 4-year term, violating the suggested requirement that a country has experienced at least one peaceful change of power in the past twenty years. Furthermore, his 1994 election was tainted by fraud and violence, allegedly the second such time this has occurred (Morley, 1994).

The Venezuelan government formally suspended some key civil liberties, such as the constitutional prohibition against searches and arrests without warrants. In recognition thereof, even the usually tolerant Freedom House rating lowered Venezuela's status from "free" to "partly free" ("Venezuela Suspends," 1994). Furthermore, its judicial system appears to be corrupt, with judges accepting payoffs in return for rendering appropriate decisions ("Another Chapter," 1995).

Freedom House also lowered its evaluation of Columbia, though for somewhat different political offenses (see "Democracy and Growth," 1994; Karatnycky, 1996). In addition, freedom of the press is considerably compromised by corruption, by governmental efforts to have the media present positive news, and the like ("Latin America's Freeish Press," 1995).

While Ecuador is rated as a democracy, violations of human rights have occurred in the near past and the military is looked at as a threat to rights in the future ("The Army," 1993). The 1995 Freedom House rating has Ecuador as a free country—but one that is beginning to slide downward (Karatnycky, 1996).

Jamaica is generally accepted as a democracy. Nonetheless, questions arise about the extent of governmental corruption, semicollusive party competition, and a resulting low voter turnout rate ("New Politricks," 1995).

The classification of Brazil and Argentina as democracies is at least debatable ("Latin America's Freeish Press," 1995; Karatnycky, 1996), although Argentina has just enjoyed its third consecutive free presidential election—a record for this country ("Back to Work," 1995). According to Freedom House, Bolivia has fallen to only partly free, losing its designation as a democratic state (Karatnycky, 1996).

Peru is another dubious case. Its constitution has lately been suspended by President Fujimori ("Fujimoriland," 1994; Karatnycky, 1996) and Fujimori has overridden the courts and granted amnesty to soldiers and police accused of violating citizens' civil liberties ("Glimmering Path," 1995).

Asia

India is another problematic case. First, of course, it flirted with authoritarianism under Indira Gandhi. Second, one party has ruled for most of this country's independent existence since World War II (our definition specifies competing parties and meaningful elections). While one-party democracy theoretically can be justified, on balance, this works against accountability and responsiveness to the citizenry. Third, fraud has been rampant in elections (Hazarika, 1994; "The Revolt," 1993). Fourth, both State Department accounts and Amnesty International reports indicate widespread acts against political freedom by the government (Potter, 1993:368). Fifth, freedom of religion, whatever its formal status, has yet to be meaningfully assured in practice. Finally, central government rule over the province of Kashmir has raised questions about both civil rights and free elections ("Guns and Votes," 1995; "Trapped," 1995).

There is some question about according democratic status to the Philippines. South Korea, where incautious praise of North Korea can lead to prosecution, has a spotty record on human rights ("National Insecurity," 1994). Its notorious National Security Law remains on the books ("The Civilian Emperor," 1995); labor leaders were arrested by the government because the state did not like the union's position on privatization ("Not So Militant," 1995). Still, gains are being made in free elections ("South Korea's Local Heroes," 1995).[9]

Other Considerations

Finally, there is the previously mentioned matter of stability. Over a 10-year period, according to Gastil's figures (Gastil, 1991), no less than ten of the countries on this initial short list have moved in or out of democratic status at least once.

If we question some of the "three-vote" choices, fairness dictates that we take an equally careful look at those governments that received only two votes, thus barely missing the short list. The "two cheers for democracy" nations were:

Czechoslovakia (now divided, of course, into the Czech Republic and Slovakia)
Hungary
Poland
Sri Lanka
Thailand

There are some sizeable problems here, too. Democracy in Thailand seems to be on a downward path, with Freedom House lowering its 1991 classification of "free" to "partly free" two years later; the 1995 rating by Freedom House remained at only partly free (Karatnycky, 1996). Indeed, its politics are characterized as corrupt ("Hucksters on the Hustings," 1995; "More Cash than Dash," 1995; "Thailand's Frail Democracy," 1995). Sri Lanka has problems with both elections and observance of individual rights (Karatnycky, 1996), not to mention routine censorship of the media ("Muzzling the Press," 1995).

On the other hand, the "two-vote" status does less than full justice, we submit, to Poland, Hungary, and what is now the Czech Republic. These are admittedly quite young and possibly not yet fully tested. Still, on the basis of the two criteria used as touchstones, a plausible case can be made that each deserves inclusion on the short list.[10]

The Short, Short List

This brings us, finally, to those countries that we think can safely be labeled as democracies today, keeping in mind the widely accepted two key requirements: (1) majority rule involving free and open elections, and (2) protection of civil liberties by a reasonably independent judiciary. Based on the foregoing discussion, and (to repeat) excluding the microstates, we would offer the following honor roll of what, for want of a better term, we call the democratic "macronations":

Australia	Israel
Austria	Italy
Belgium	Jamaica
Botswana	Japan
Canada	Netherlands
Costa Rica	New Zealand
Czech Republic	Norway
Denmark	Poland
Ecuador	Portugal
Finland	Spain
France	Sweden
Germany	Switzerland
Greece	United Kingdom
Hungary	United States
Ireland	

Are there countries that should be on this list and have not been included? We do not think so. We have, in fact, added Hungary, the Czech Republic, and Poland despite their failure to receive the requisite number of "votes" in the studies on which we have relied. Their recent emergence as democracies and apparent acceptance of civil liberties make them worthy nominees to this company.

Some readers, no doubt, will insist that we have erred in omitting India. For the reasons advanced earlier we would argue otherwise. Frankly, we see this as an easy designation; India misses by a wide margin.

Are there countries on the list that should not be there? As of this writing, we have some doubts about Ecuador. Almost every reader, we anticipate, will have similar misgivings about one country or another. But the addition or subtraction of a nation or two, or even two or three, will not significantly alter the conclusions to which this list points. That being the case, we will take it as it stands, whatever our personal reservations.[11]

Now That They Have Been Identified . . .

Our roster of democratic polities, with very minor modifications, has been based on the classifications made in six separate studies—plus recent developments. Almost all of these studies use many of the same evaluative criteria, their authors are manifestly prodemocratic (as we are), and, possibly because of this, several have been quite generous in their categorizations, as the examples we mentioned attest. This generosity notwithstanding, all of the studies—even Vanhanen's—make it clear that democracies still constitute a modest minority of present day governments.[12] Of the 148 macro-nations, only 28 (or 19 percent) can reasonably be said to fall under this heading.[13]

Freedom House ratings from 1995 provide yet one more means of looking at this matter. Their criterion for free countries is, essentially, the two-pronged definition already discussed. Table 1, based on their criteria, makes interesting reading (Karatnycky, 1996:3):

Table 1
Freedom in the World: Percentage of World Population Living under Different Types of Political Systems

Year	Free	Partly Free	Not Free
January 1981	35.9	21.6	42.5
January 1984	36.0	23.0	41.0
January 1987	37.1	23.6	39.3
January 1990	38.9	21.9	39.3
January 1993	24.8	44.1	31.1
January 1996	19.6	41.5	39.0

What is especially poignant is that the percentage of humans living under free governments, by Freedom House's own reckoning, has plummeted over the past decade and a half. Overall, the proportion of citizens living under "not free" governments has declined only modestly. The growth area is "partly free" societies. It thus appears as though we have had some decay of free societies toward partly free—if Freedom House's figures are accepted as valid.

Furthermore, despite two world wars fought to "make the world safe for democracy," the ratio of democracies to nondemocracies has remained little changed for some 75 years (Dahl, 1991:77). As Huntington (1991, 1991–1992) has shown, there have been several democratic waves over the past century, with the number of democratic polities increasing—and then diminishing. Of the newly created post–World War I democracies, few survived even into the mid-1930s; nor did many established after World War II long endure.[14]

More recently, the collapse of the USSR gave rise to numerous freshly minted independent states that were promptly hailed as "democracies" or, by those just a bit more cautious, as "proto democracies" (Nelson and Bentley, 1994). But both Huntington's historical perspective and, even more saddening, political developments in many of these nations, warrant the fear that few of them are likely to justify either of these designations by the end of this century.

In short, the roster of sovereign nations has expanded, at least for the time being. Nonetheless, the long-standing pattern has altered little, if at all—authoritarian states still constitute a very substantial majority, and democracies still a relatively small minority, of political societies. And that is precisely what a dispassionate observer, familiar with our social primate evolutionary legacy, surely would have predicted.

Beyond doubt, ours is a species predisposed by its social primate origins to hierarchical, rather than democratic, governance. We turn now to the specific behavioral tendencies (and the reasons for their evolution) that make this the general rule but, given one of Homo sapiens' very unique attributes, also permit occasional exceptions.

NOTES

1. In this case, *The American Political Dictionary* (Plano and Greenberg, 1993:8–9).

2. See, for example, Dahl (1971, 1989); Vanhanen (1984, 1990); Bobbio (1987); Gastil (1991); Bollen (1991, 1993).

3. This is plainly a much less demanding definition than that, say, of Polybius, who insists, in addition, on "a reverence to the gods, honor for parents, respect to others, [and] obedience to laws as traditional and habitual." Herbert Werlin would also require "a mutual respect among competing leaders and followers." (1994:530). Both men, surely by contemporary standards, are much too exiguous.

4. In some instances, to be sure, there may be an interim appointment to fill out an unexpired term.

5. The faith was not quite unlimited, since women were not allowed to participate in political decision making. Nor were slaves, who constituted about a third of the Athenian population.

6. A few Italian Renaissance city-states, such as Florence, could possibly be added to the list. However, these were small-scale polities, encompassing both small areas and small populations. Furthermore, these so-called republics were mixed in nature, with the "people" being only one of several constituent groups involved in governance. See, for instance, Held, 1993. A wonderful book, edited by R. W. Davis, outlines the origins of modern free states in the West—and indicates the problems with confidently saying that, for instance, Italian city-state republics were good democracies in action (Davis, 1995).

7. These are: (1) the percentage of citizens actually voting in the nation's elections; and (2) the smaller parties' share of the vote (the larger their share, he reasons, presumably the more democratic the country).

8. Here is a roster of the microstates, those countries with a population of less than one million people (those deemed democracies are given a "D" in parentheses):

Andorra (D)	Maldives
Antigua and Barbuda	Malta (D)
Bahamas (D)	Marshall Islands (D)
Bahrain	Micronesia (D)
Barbados (D)	Monaco
Belize (D)	Nauru (D)
Brunei	Qatar
Cape Verde	St. Kitts-Nevis (D)
Comoros	St. Lucia (D)
Cyprus	St. Vincent (D)
Djibouti	San Marino (D)
Dominica (D)	Sao Tome and Principe
Equitorial Guinea	Seychelles
Fiji (D)	Solomon Islands (D)
Gambia	Suriname
Grenada (D)	Swaziland
Guyana	Tonga
Iceland (D)	Tuvalu (D)
Kiribati (D)	Vanuatu (D)
Liechtenstein (D)	Western Samoa (D)
Luxembourg (D)	

Some of those countries that we have deemed democratic, in fact, are hardly pristine. We were somewhat reluctant, for instance, to judge Fiji and the Bahamas as democratic, given a recent record of violating rights of unpopular ethnic/racial groupings (e.g., see Rohter, 1994; "Second Thoughts," 1994).

9. While many claim that Japan is one of the world's leading democracies, that listing is at least open to some skepticism. First, the Liberal party was the lone

party to rule for most of Japan's existence as a democracy. Second, corruption is widespread among government leaders. Third, the Liberal party's oligarchy normally handpicks the head of government. Finally, respect for individual rights is not as deeply rooted as in other Western democracies ("The Secret, 1994; Sterngold, 1994). Chalmers Johnson (quoted in Sorenson, 1993:17) observes:

Since 1947, despite its adoption of a formally democratic constitution and the subsequent development of a genuinely open political culture, Japan seems to have retained many "soft authoritarian" features in its governmental institutions: an extremely strong and comparatively unsupervised state administration, single-party rule for more than three decades, and a set of economic priorities that seems unattainable under true political pluralism during such a long period.

In the end, we counted Japan as a democracy. Nonetheless, there is at least some ambiguity, as just noted.

10. For completeness, we should also identify the crypto-democracies, that is, those countries named only once (in the six enumerations) as a democracy. They are: Albania, Armenia, Bulgaria, Chile, El Salvador, Gambia, Ghana, Guatemala, Latvia, Lebanon, Liberia, Lithuania, Malaysia, Mexico, Namibia, Nicaragua, Pakistan, Panama, Singapore, Sudan, Turkey, and Zambia.

That some of these states were ranked even once as democracies is surprising. Others may have a slightly better claim but, by and large, few will question the conclusion that there are no real democracies among these "one-vote" governments. The strongest claimants would be the Baltic states, Latvia and Lithuania; you might also be able to make a case for Chile.

11. Some readers will doubtless protest that we are much too stringent in our willingness to declare a specific country democratic. However, we would counter that the term "democracy" is debased by willy-nilly applying the title to countries that have serious problems with civil liberties or routinely rig elections.

Serious discourse on the subject of democracy requires that we take this term seriously and set a sensible standard for using it. Otherwise, the concept becomes little more than a mirage. We suspect that many who are willing to call dubious candidate countries democracies do so out of an understandable desire to believe that, to paraphrase a line from the song in the musical *Carousel*, "Democracy is busting out all over."

12. Even *The Economist*, which somehow manages to find "freedom" in the most unexpected—we are tempted to say unbelievable—places, classified only 74 of 184 (macro- and microstates) as "free" (August 27, 1994, p. 16). A more critical evaluation, we think it fair to say, would have cut the figure by more than half.

13. Even if we add some of what we see as possible borderline cases (the Baltic states, Chile, Argentina), the enumeration reaches only 33 out of 148 macrostates, or 22 percent.

If we wished, we could recalculate, adding into the equation countries that we see as promising at this point but not yet, in our judgment, even quite at the level of the five countries just noted. Among these might be South Korea, Uruguay,

Mauritius, Slovenia, South Africa, Cyprus, Malawi, Mali. But the fundamental point remains the same: the clear majority of large nations is not democratic.

14. This may be the appropriate place to point out that historical evidence does not suggest that democracies have longer life spans than nondemocracies. In a study of countries carried out over a long time span, Gurr (1974) reports that the average polity lasts only about 32 years. There is little indication from his evidence that democracy is any more stable than other governmental forms.

Part III

The Neo-Darwinian Case and Supporting Evidence

Chapter 5

Dominance and Hierarchy

The absence of inequality and of dominance (i.e., the presence of equality and nondominance) is a theoretical possibility that is apparently not encountered empirically in human society.

Gerald D. Berreman, *Social Inequality*, 1981

INTRODUCTION

In one way, evolution has been generous to the social primates, for they are surely the most intelligent of all species. From a democratic perspective, though, evolution has been less kind, since they have also been endowed with an innate predisposition for dominance relations between individuals and for hierarchical social structures characterized by distinct differences of rank and status.

As social primates, humans share this evolutionary legacy, one that carries with it considerable political baggage. This genetic heritage, we submit, constitutes a (probably even *the)* major obstacle to the emergence and survival of democratic government. Dominance and hierarchy do not easily accord, history testifies, with the basic democratic ideals of political equality, majority rule, and equality before the law.

In this chapter, we begin with the reasons why dominance relationships evolve in a social species— that is, with the benefits that, on balance, accrue to the individual (and conceivably the collective) members of that species from these behaviors. Those familiar with evolutionary theory as it applies to social behavior may well choose to skip this relatively brief exposition and move directly to the section on "Hierarchy," later in the chapter.

Social primates display dominance behavior; in every instance so far observed, they also live in hierarchical social (and in the case of our species, political) structures. Hierarchy is, in fact, one of the most pervasive and ubiquitous characteristics of human social (as well as political) organization, a theme to which the second section of this chapter is devoted. No less than dominance, this inclination constitutes a formidable obstacle to democratic governance.

DOMINANCE

Dominance is normally defined as a relationship between two members of the same species in which there is a high probability that the dominant animal will have preferential access to some good to which both animals aspire.[1] The desired good may be of almost any sort—food, shelter, a reproductive partner, a territory, a preferred seating place, and, by no means least of all, deference.

Two male chimpanzees, for example, may come simultaneously upon a trove of bananas. Both are hungry and both want to eat the bananas, but the dominant chimpanzee, either automatically or by simply a threatening gesture, will have prior access; the subordinate will eat only after the dominant has consented or finished—if any of the food remains.

Dominance is achieved in a variety of ways, depending upon the species and the specific situation. Taking the animal kingdom as a whole, actual physical combat is perhaps the least common method, since it carries with it the danger of serious injury or even death to one or even both of the contestants. More frequently, dominance is established by threat and display, with the smaller or less formidable looking individual yielding to a larger or more fearsome opponent. This outcome benefits both participants: for the dominant, there is no physical risk; for the subordinate, the short-term loss of status and/or access to a desired good may well be offset, in the long run, by the opportunity to grow older, stronger, and more fearsome—and perhaps eventually to reverse the relationship.

Interestingly enough, though hardly surprising from a human perspective, dominance among many social species is sometimes achieved by inheritance. Where this occurs, as with chimpanzees,[2] the offspring take on a status either equal to, or just a step below, the status of their mother; that is, they will normally be dominant to (most of) those chimpanzees (and their offspring) who are subordinate to her and subordinate to those chimpanzees (and their progeny) who are superior to her. We say "normally" because it is quite possible for the son or daughter of a low-ranking mother to move markedly upward in the group's social hierarchy (that is, to become dominant over those to whom he or she was previously subordinate) by some combination of threat, force, and alliance.

As the foregoing suggests, alliance with one or more fellow con-specifics is yet another technique for achieving a more dominant status. The making and breaking of these alliances among chimpanzees, graphically described by Frans de Waal (1989; see also Harcourt and de Waal, 1992) sometimes reaches a level of malevolent sophistication that Machiavelli himself might admire.

The Evolutionary Benefits of Dominance

According to neo-Darwinian theory, an individual should behave in such a way as to maximize the number of his/her genes transmitted to the next generation. This can be done in two different ways: First, by passing along one's genes directly, usually referred to as individual reproductive success. Second, one can behave in such a manner as to increase reproductive success of one's relatives, with whom one shares genes (Barash, 1982). The combination of these two is termed "inclusive fitness," encompassing the reproductive success both of an individual and of that individual's relatives with whom, depending upon the degree of relatedness, the individual shares more or fewer genes (Barash, 1982).[3]

In any species, accordingly, the individual should behave in such a way as to maximize the number of his or her genes appearing in the next generation. Since relatives share genes, there is some (usually unconscious, of course) motivation for that individual to invest energy in also enhancing the reproductive success of relatives. This is the conceptual framework, then, that enables us to understand the role played by dominance behavior and hierarchy formation in the process of natural selection.

Darwinian theory holds that when a given behavior is consistently manifested by a species, or by a number of related species, there is probably a sound evolutionary reason for that behavior.[4] When we consider that all of the social primates exhibit dominance behavior, we can reasonably hypothesize that this behavior must contribute, directly or indirectly, to the reproductive success and inclusive fitness of the members of these species.

It takes no great leap of imagination, therefore, to conclude that dominance behavior has evolved among the social primates because it enhances the individual's reproductive success and/or inclusive fitness. We find substantial evidence for this among baboons (Dixson, Bossi, and Wickings, 1993; Packer et al., 1995), macaques (Paul and Kuester, 1990; Smith, 1993; Bauers and Hearn, 1994; de Ruiter, van Hooff, and Scheffrahn, 1994), and chimpanzees (Ely, Alford, and Ferrell, 1991), to mention only a few of the primate species that have been studied.[5]

Another way in which dominance behavior affects reproductive opportunities has already been suggested. Dominance relations yield predictability. Individuals know where they stand with one another with respect to access to valued resources, as noted earlier.[6] As a consequence, there is no need constantly to dispute who is to get what, disputes which, at best, would entail repeated and possibly substantial investments of energy and, at worst, repeated risks of injury or death.

Dominance furthers predictability, and predictability, in turn, benefits both the dominant and the subordinate. The former gains the desired resource (and resulting possible enhancement of inclusive fitness) at no greater cost than a possible threat or two; the subordinate, by yielding, escapes a clash that might otherwise reduce or literally end his or her reproductive possibilities.

No less significantly, a society beset with continuing turmoil is not conducive to reproductive success. The more orderly mode of life generated by the type of predictability just described creates more felicitous conditions for passing one's genes along to the next generation. A stable, peaceful society is more apt to lead to individual reproductive success than one in continuing disarray and upheaval as a result of constant fighting over status and resources.

Dominance, we should emphasize, is not necessarily a purely individual characteristic. True, in simple, small, primate societies, dominance relations usually lead to "linear" hierarchies, with each animal ranked from top (alpha) to bottom (omega). But in more complex societies, as previously mentioned, several animals may unite together in an alliance or coalition so that they rank at the top—even though some of them might otherwise rank quite low purely on the basis of dyadic (one-to-one, simple dominance) relations.[7] Dominance hierarchies in these societies, consequently, are not simply the sum of all dyadic relations.

However, whether a society is characterized by a linear hierarchy or by a more complex coalition structure, the net result is essentially the same in evolutionary terms. Hierarchy leads to social stability, and this stability, on balance, is conducive to more successful reproduction among the members of that society. Hierarchy and social stability, an outgrowth of dominance relations among a social species, function to enhance the likelihood that the individuals who constitute that species will maximize their inclusive fitness. The direct benefit is to the individual—but the group and, presumably, ultimately the species may itself also gain thereby.[8]

From a neo-Darwinian perspective, and whether considered solely from the benefits to the individual or, conceivably to the group or species, that is why hierarchical social structures evolved among social primates as a consistent and significant component of their behavioral repertoire. And, as with our social primate relatives, so, too, with humans.

HIERARCHY: THE THIRD CERTAINTY

> The tradition of inequality is, so to say, a complex—a cluster of ideas at the back of men's minds, whose influence they do not like to admit but which, nevertheless, determines their outlook on society . . . their practical conduct, and the direction of their policy.
>
> R. H. Tawney, *Equality*, 1931

> The great paradox of the modern world is that everywhere men attach themselves to the principle of equality and everywhere, in their own lives, as well as in the lives of others, they encounter the presence of inequality.
>
> Andre Beteille, *Inequality among Men*, 1977

"In this world," runs Ben Franklin's most often quoted aphorism, "nothing is certain but death and taxes." True—but not quite the whole truth. Where there are humans, there is a third certainty—hierarchy.[9]

Democracies have been rare, our thesis holds, because we are genetically predisposed toward authoritarian social structures. The logic of this argument obviously requires that the same predisposition for hierarchical organizations be found operative not only in the political realm but in practically every aspect of our species' social life. The purpose of this section of the chapter is to persuade—or remind—the reader that such is precisely the case.

Hierarchy—Ubiquitous, Ineluctable

There is something paradoxical, if not ironic, about the need to demonstrate the universality among humans of hierarchical structures embodying marked differences of status, benefits, and privilege, or of the manifold material and psychological gains and losses that are associated with these differences. Of all social phenomena, hierarchy is the most pervasive; for almost all of us, the major and minor events of our existence occur within, and are shaped by, one hierarchy or another. This was true in the past; as Joseph Shepher notes, it is equally the case today (Shepher, 1987:174):

Modern human life is basically a study in dominance hierarchies: we spend most of our waking hours in hierarchies that range from corporate industry to government administration, from supermarkets to department stores, from the elementary school to the university. Even our clubs, associations, churches, and hospitals are hierarchically organized, all displaying a wide variety of dominance systems. . . . [M]odern adolescents can hardly find a more important system to adjust to than dominance hierarchies.

Shepher's last point is especially important. If dominance hierarchies are omnipresent, so, too, are status distinctions. As might be expected of Homo sapiens, the social primate par excellence, these distinctions "exist in groups of whatever kind, from garden clubs, to street gangs, to orchestras with soloists and dramatic conductors, to seminaries where some are holier than others and holier than thous" (Tiger, 1992:266). Randolph Nesse expressed much the same idea when he observed that "it is possible to get enough food and water, for a time, at least, but no amount of social status seems enough" (1994:343).

Even language, that transcendent tool that sets humankind apart from all other species, reflects our seemingly ineluctable tendency to create and then observe differences of rank. That is hardly surprising: according to the Noam Chomsky school of linguistics, these deep-structure language communalities are literally rooted in the anatomical structure and physiological functioning of the brain (Chomsky, 1972). Practically all languages abound in honorifics and in pronouns that recognize and reinforce status distinctions (*Sie, Du*, avoidance of the direct "you" in speaking to a superior, etc.); in some languages verbs, too, are modified for the same purpose.

Despite—or more likely because of—the manner in which hierarchy permeates our social existence, students of human behavior have been surprisingly slow to grasp its pervasiveness. The reason, according to Louis Dumont, who has written extensively on the subject, is that "Modern man [*sic*] is virtually incapable of fully recognizing [hierarchy]. If it does force itself on his attention, he tends to eliminate it as an epiphenomenon" (1966:xvii). Dumont may be correct; it is usually very difficult to take adequate cognizance of that which is totally familiar.[10] In any event, even when its importance is recognized, we have been slow to understand hierarchy's evolutionary origins and significance.

The initial explanations for the universality of hierarchy and of status differentiations were, and by most social scientists probably still are, cast in purely sociological terms, social learning, separate invention, and cultural diffusion, borrowing and imitation. Although theoretically conceivable, it is highly improbable that social learning can even begin adequately to account for the regularity and similarity of dominance structures and dominance-related behaviors among peoples separated by vast distances of time, space, and cultural development. Instead, as Tiger and Fox argued in one of the first full-scale neo-Darwinian challenges to the long-accepted sociological wisdom,

in this business of being inferior and superior, we do not begin from scratch but rather draw on an elaborate repertoire of already programmed ways of showing those differences of status it seems we are compelled to show. The inflexible and consistent connection of all this with the way we evolved as a breeding species confirms our connection with our own prehistory (1971:41–42).

More recently, Benson Ginsburg—to cite only one of many other examples of the neo-Darwinian perspective[11]—has expressed the same idea, albeit more briefly and conservatively:

All [human] groups have their dominance-deference hierarchies. Collectively and historically, such hierarchical organizations appear to be rooted in the biological nature of our species, and must, therefore, be, in part, understood in evolutionary terms. (1988:1)[12]

THE COUNTERARGUMENTS

Three basic objections will undoubtedly occur to those who are reluctant or simply unwilling to acknowledge the possible influence of biological factors on human behavior.

Hierarchy as Socially Learned

The first and most familiar objection is that children are naturally egalitarian and that their subsequent manifestation of hierarchical behavior is best understood as the product of learning and social emulation. Unfortunately, this is simply not the case. Status distinctions, child ethologists have consistently found, speedily and spontaneously emerge even in groups of very young children. When children are put together, they immediately begin to form hierarchies.[13] Some become leaders, others are acquiescent. Leaders' strategies include hedonic (praise, nonthreatening verbalizations) and agonic (threats or actual use of force) behaviors, the very same tactics used by the young of other social primates.[14]

The Argument from "Natural Man"

One of the most attractive and cherished notions in social philosophy maintains that, in the "state of nature," our remote ancestors lived in a truly egalitarian and harmonious manner.[15] According to this theory, differences in social and political status, the vast disparities in wealth, the resort to violence and war—in brief, the shortcomings of society as we know it, are afflictions springing from the insidiously corrupting influence of private property and of the state.

From such a perspective, "natural man" is seen, almost by definition, as inherently egalitarian and democratic. This theory both predicts and requires, then, that peoples still living in a state of nature display these appealing characteristics.

Plainly, there are serious difficulties here. First, that of actually finding such a people.[16] As the world daily grows more crowded, the likelihood that there still exist such societies becomes increasingly minuscule. Furthermore, no matter how skilled and careful the observer, there is the problem of accurately describing, through twentieth-century eyes, a world so staggeringly different from our own.

Third, even should they be found, the initial contact with such a people often sets profound change into motion, since it automatically ends the geographic and cultural isolation that (presumably) left the group so quintessentially "primitive." Small wonder that anthropologists and sociologists have differed among themselves in what they see, even though their respective visits may have taken place within relatively brief intervals of time. Allowing for all of this, studies of what are now called "hunter-gatherers" may still cast some light on the matter, for their way of life may be[17] the way our forefathers lived during much of our species' evolution.

Until well into the twentieth century, many of those who studied these societies often described a halcyon, peaceful egalitarian mode of life. This notion, in fact, became practically an article of faith. Surveying the literature on this issue, Flanagan tartly observed that "much of the work reviewed here is written from a committed stance. . . . The dominant mode of anthropological theorizing since the 19th century has treated egalitarianism as a sort of evolutionary starting point, with evolutionary social differentiation leading inevitably to hierarchy"(1989:248, 260). In a similar vein, Myers complained of the "ideological use" of the earlier "hunter-gatherer" studies (1988:264).

Over the past few decades, however, quite another picture began to emerge, as perhaps more objective observers reported unmistakable patterns of dominance and submission (for example, Lee and DeVore, 1968). Just like Margaret Mead's heartwarming myth of casual, guilt-free sex in Samoa, the earlier, idyllic portrayals of natural man in the state of nature are no longer tenable.

Of late, anthropologists, sociologists, and human ethologists have come to distinguish between "immediate-return" and "delayed-return" primitive societies.[18] The former, exceedingly rare, quite small (say, thirty to fifty members), and commonly little more than extended families, are characterized by very simple tools and, as the term suggests, by the immediate consumption of food. Even in these societies, though, there are observable, if comparatively modest, status differences. When, for whatever reason, these become oppressive, the group simply fissions into two or more entities.

The much more common delayed return societies, on the other hand, will store food for future consumption,[19] are considerably larger; were probably initially created by the aggregation of distinct families that often still constitute their components, have more advanced tools, and recognize property rights. As the foregoing suggests, these societies display in rich abundance and variety the social stratification and other inequalities with which we are so familiar (Woodburn, 1980, 1982).

In both types of society, though, we find the same underlying, pyramidal structure: modest but unmistakable patterns of dominance and submission in the former,[20] greater and considerably sharper differences of status in the latter. The presently prevailing view, consequently, is that "no society or family system anywhere in the world has ever been egalitarian" (van den Berghe, 1980:72); that "few, if any societies are without some form of domination, whether it is based on age, gender, kinship, or some more institutionalized form of domination" (Hendricks, 1988:216); that "all known human societies have some form of social inequality, even those labelled by the ethnographic literature as 'egalitarian'" (Aldenderfer, 1993:1);[21] and that "there are no societies totally lacking hierarchy" (Goldberg, 1993:16).[22] To which we should add Flanagan's wry caveat, "nor . . . are there any simple societies" (1989:261).

The Utopian Challenge

The third objection (actually concerned more with the implications, rather than the validity, of our thesis) comes from those usually called "utopians." Is it not possible, they ask, that human wisdom can design a society in which (1) if hierarchical social life is a learned behavior, it will *not* be learned, or (2) even if hierarchy is an innate tendency, the society will be so cleverly constructed that it will provide little or no opportunity for the tendency to manifest itself?

To this question, two answers are possible, one dealing with theory, the other with practice. With regard to the former, yes: it is conceivable that, once behavioral science has attained a clearer understanding of the interplay between the evolutionary and the socially transmitted wellsprings of human behavior, such a society might be (in fact, is almost certain to be) designed—on paper. There will still remain, however, the small problem that has plagued all utopian schemes from Plato on—how do we get from here to there? To this, no solution has yet been forthcoming.

As far as practice is concerned, the response is hardly encouraging. The nature of utopian undertakings, we know, has varied greatly. Some of these communities were based, from their very inception, on an inequality of status; others, though, sought to establish societies that were economically and politically egalitarian. Lamentably, few of these attempts to build a better world, of whatever type, survived more than a decade or two. Of those utopias that endured for any notable length of time, all were either authoritarian by intent or, if not so originally, soon developed marked differences of authority and influence.[23]

Elitist Political Theory

As those familiar with the history of Western political philosophy know, there is nothing novel in the claim that political structures are invariably hierarchical and that, in all polities, the many are ruled by the few. The desirability of such an arrangement, in fact, had been advocated by Plato and Aristotle, by the monarchists, by Luther and Calvin, and later by Hegel, Burke, Carlyle, even Kant,[24] to mention only some of the more illustrious names. As the nineteenth century drew to a close, though, the so-called elitist political philosophers (Mosca, Pareto, and Michels are undoubtedly the best known) approached the issue in quite a different fashion.

Rule by the few, they insisted, was neither a matter of desirability nor of choice—it was simply inevitable.[25] In Michels's famous formulation (1915), this became the "Iron Law of Oligarchy"; for Mosca (1939), it was the "ruling class"; and with Pareto (1935), the "elite." For all three, change in governments involve (and can only involve) a change in the composition of the ruling oligarchy, class, or elite. It followed, then, that democracy, in any meaningful egalitarian sense, was an unattainable illusion. All three men, too, insisted that this pessimistic prophecy was an objective, scientific judgment, not an expression of personal preference.[26]

What makes the elitists particularly germane to this discussion is the evidence that purportedly led them to their conclusions. All of them relied, implicitly or explicitly, on the argument from history, that is, "It has always been this way, consequently, it will always be." Michels (1915), in addition, brought to bear the argument from organizational necessity—that is, (1) the pursuit of any political objective requires political organization; (2) those who head the organization will use their positions to benefit themselves to the detriment of the organization's membership and at the cost of its original professed collective objectives; (3) since the incumbent leaders command the organization's resources, they are usually successful in that effort; (4) in the relatively rare instances where the leaders can be ousted, they are simply replaced by a new oligarchy that in short order yields to the same temptations; (5) all the while, the rank and file actually accept this state of affairs, since this spares them the necessity of allocating their spare time to the odious chores of organizational involvement.[27]

This brings us full circle, for both the argument from organizational necessity and the argument from history are based on a given conception of human nature. In so doing, to be sure, the elitists were following a firmly established tradition. The nature of human nature has been the point of departure for every major political theorist; it has been the "most fundamental question of all" (Berelson and Steiner, 1964:662) in political philosophy from its very inception.[28] Still, despite the centrality of the issue, neither the elitists nor any other school of thought could offer a convincing reason *why* human nature was as they claimed it to be. Politically, the elitists insisted, humans were "naturally" (and inevitably) hierarchical—but they could go no further.

Now, for the first time, neo-Darwinism affords a credible explanation for the persistence and prevalence of political systems almost always embodying the rule of a relative few. In that respect, it provides a cogent explanation, as well as critical supporting evidence, for the elitists' interpretation of the political past and the political present. Beyond that point, though, the two part company. An evolutionary perspective also carries with it the possibility—and it is admittedly no more than that—of a political future different from that predicted by the elitists.

Before we turn to that possibility, however, we must discuss a logical corollary of hierarchy, an inherent willingness to obey. The next chapter, then, deals with that subject. Then, to complete our discussion of the manner in which evolution has influenced our social and political behavior, we look at the remarkable trait with which our species alone has been endowed—indoctrinability. To be sure, indoctrinability can, and as we have previously observed, usually does reinforce our genetic predispositions toward authoritarian governance. Nonetheless, it is this unique capacity that also enables us to accept and to act in behalf of ideals and values that run counter to our innate tendencies. That, in the final analysis, is what makes democracy sometimes viable.

NOTES

1. "An animal may be said to be dominant if it has a high probability of winning hostile encounters" (Moyer, 1987:2). For various approaches to dominance, see Bernstein (1981), Jolly (1985), Walters and Seyfarth (1987).

2. This is also the pattern with macaques (Koford, 1963; Eaton, 1976; Berman, 1986) and baboons (Hausfater, Altmann, and Altmann, 1982). There is so far little evidence of this among gorillas (Stewart and Harcourt, 1987). We should note that there can be evolution-based differences in behavior among relatively closely related species, for instance *Pan troglodytes* versus bonobos among chimpanzees.

3. Put in more formal terms, inclusive fitness is "the sum of an individual's fitness as measured by reproductive success and that of relatives, with those relatives devalued in proportion to their genetic distance, i.e., as they share fewer genes" (Barash, 1982:392).

4. In Robert Frank's succinct phrase, "the physical characteristics and even the behavior of a species evolve in such ways as to give individual members of the species the greatest reproductive advantage" (1985:132). For earlier, classic expositions of neo-Darwinism, see Simpson (1944, 1953) and Mayr (1970). For more recent treatments, see Maynard-Smith (1982), Levinton (1988), Plotkin (1988), and Dawkins (1989b).

5. However, some questions on this have recently been raised by Ellis (1995).

6. To complicate matters, one animal may be subordinate to another with respect to one resource, such as food, and dominant over that same animal with respect to another resource, such as a preferred sleeping area (Jolly, 1985). Some contend that dominance should not be defined in terms of access to resources but rather as "approach-withdrawal" behavior (Walters and Seyfarth, 1987).

7. For an excellent example of this among savanna baboons, see Hall and DeVore's (1965) story of old Kovu, low ranking in dyadic dominance relations but near the top of the hierarchy because of his association with more powerful allies.

8. Until quite recently, orthodox neo-Darwinian theory held that natural selection and, consequently, evolution operated purely at the individual and not at the group or species level. For changing opinions on this issue, see Wilson and Sober (1994) and Wilson (1995).

9. In fact, it is even more certain than taxes. Among very "primitive" peoples we may not find taxes, but we will assuredly find hierarchy.

10. "In a way, it's not surprising that the rediscovery of human nature has taken us so long. Being everywhere we look, it tends to elude us" (Wright, 1994:8).

11. For a detailed exposition of this view by the best known of contemporary ethologists, see Eibl-Eibesfeldt, 1989.

12. Ridley (1994:119) reduced the proposition to a single sentence: "humans are a highly social species whose society is nearly always stratified in some way."

13. See, for example, Strayer and Strayer (1976), Barner-Barry (1977, 1981), Hold (1977, 1980). Edelman and Omark (1973) report on the stability of these distinctions. Similar findings were reported by Omark and Edelman (1975), and Pickert and Wall (1981).

14. "More evidence on the fundamental similarity between hierarchical relationships among subadult humans and among nonhuman animals has come from comparing dominance signals" (Ellis, 1993:28).

15. For a detailed demolition of what the author calls "the myth of the peaceful savage," see Keeley (1996).

16. For a case study, see Gordon (1992) on whether the bushmen (!Kung) are (or were) truly primitive.

17. As students are repeatedly warned, the hunter-gatherer societies surviving in the ethnographic present may be quite different from those of earlier ages.

18. This terminology (Woodburn, 1979, 1980; Ingold, Riches, and Woodburn, 1988) was quite similar to the distinctions between "instantaneous return" and "deferred distribution" societies previously drawn by Meillassoux (1973).

19. One anthropologist sees this as the critical point of differentiation, and speaks of the "profoundly inegalitarian nature of hunter-gatherer societies once they began to store food" (Testart, 1988:5). For discussions of this point, see Bishop (1989); Headland and Reid (1989), Gardner (1991), and Layton et al. (1991).

20. In a subsection entitled "The Dynamics of Egalitarian Foraging Societies," one of the contributors explicitly states that "leadership in the band is apparent at all phases of decision-making" (Silberman, 1982:29).

21. Needless to say, there are still those who disagree. Thus, Mansbridge claimed that hunter-gatherers "lived as equals" (1980:101), Knauft holds that there is a "relative absence" of stratification among true primitives (1991:391), and Boehm (1993) seems to feel there is a total absence. But Boehm fails to identify the societies he has in mind and, in referring to these unidentified entities, speaks of their "leaders."

22. Though working from a quite different orientation, Sahlins (1958:1) had arrived at the same conclusion quite a bit earlier, writing that

theoretically, an egalitarian society would be one in which every individual is of equal status, a society in which no one outranks any one else. But even the most primitive societies cannot be described as egalitarian in this sense. There are differences in status carrying differential privileges in every human organization.

23. According to Dolgoff (1974), some degree of equality could be found in a number of rural anarchist communes established during the Spanish Civil War. But this was a brief experiment, speedily ended by Franco's triumph.

24. Dahrendorf quotes Kant as saying that "inequality among men [is] a rich source of much that is evil, but also of everything that is good" (1968:12).

25. According to Boswell, Samuel Johnson had expressed much the same idea much earlier when he declared that "so far is it from true that men are naturally

equal, but that no two people can be half an hour together but the one shall acquire an evident superiority over the other" (Brady and Pottle, 1995:302).

26. Neither Mosca nor Pareto, there is ample reason to think, was especially troubled by their "findings." Michels, though, was deeply distressed by where his intellectual journey led him. Few passages in political philosophy are as moving—and as despairing—as his final paragraph:

The democratic currents of history resemble successive waves. They break ever on the same shoal. They are ever renewed. This enduring spectacle is simultaneously encouraging and depressing. When democracies have gained a certain state of development, they undergo a gradual transformation, adopting the aristocratic spirit, and in many cases also the aristo-cratic forms, against which at the outset they struggled so fiercely. Now new accusers arise to denounce the traitors; after an era of glorious combats and of inglorious power, they end by fusing with the old dominant class; whereupon once more they are in their turn attacked by fresh opponents who appeal to the name of democracy. It is probable that this cruel game will continue without end. (1915:408)

A strikingly similar passage is found in Martin Du Gard's novel, *Jean Barois* (1972:329–330):

Try as we may to bring freedom to our fellow men and to better their lot, human nature is against us. With each new generation all the old mistakes, the old injustices rear their ugly heads; it's always the same dreary struggle, the same victory of the strong over the weak.

27. Michels, it will be recalled, based his conclusions on the history of labor unions as well as that of political parties.

28. Almost every political philosophy rests on certain assumptions, whether explicit or implicit, about human nature. Recognizing this, Peter Reynolds has warned that "the nature of human nature is the last thing that behavioral science will discover, not its point of departure; and our research programs should be designed to discover it, not to assume it" (Reynolds, 1987).

Chapter 6

Obedience

One of the most striking things about the struggle for freedom from intentional control is how often it has been lacking. Many people have submitted to the most odious religious, governmental and economic controls for centuries.

B. F. Skinner, *Beyond Freedom and Dignity*, 1971

INTRODUCTION

Skinner erred in only one respect: he should have written "most" rather than "many" people. Another social scientist has commented on the same phenomenon from a somewhat different perspective, observing that "the widespread support for royalty throughout much of human history suggests the importance of considering the complicity of subjects in their own subordination" (Schwartz, 1989:270). True, the "subjects" are guilty of complicity—though only in the sense that they acted in compliance with one of Homo sapiens' preprogrammed behaviors, our "innate inclination to obey" (Eibl-Eibesfeldt, 1979:95).

As the foregoing subtly suggests, in this chapter we argue that among the most powerful and persistent of our evolutionary legacies is a readiness to give "obedience to those in authority" (Sagan and Druyan, 1992:169), a readiness hardly conducive to either the emergence or the survival of democratic governance. In support of this argument we adduce three types of evidence—neo-Darwinian evolutionary theory, human history, and experimental research findings.[1]

Before proceeding further, though, it is imperative that we make clear just what we are saying and, maybe even more important, what we are not saying. Not all obedience, we certainly agree, can reasonably be attributed solely to an evolutionarily derived predisposition. Some acts of obedience are no doubt voluntary in that we obey a law or a command because we think the action requested is right, moral, or desirable: possessing freedom of choice, we would take the action even if not commanded to do so.

In other instances, obedience is most sensibly explained in terms of threat and force. Individuals, groups, and sometimes entire populations obey because they rightly fear the consequences of disobedience. It may well be that, as we are often reassured, "stark coercion, unsupported by other devices, is usually unsuccessful over long periods of time" (Wilkinson, 1969:8). But even the most coercive regimes rarely rely on force "unsupported by other devices"; in any event, this long-term consolation may be inadequate incentive for those who risk paying the price of disobedience in the short run.

Last, obedience may flow simply from social conditioning and established habit, keeping in mind that this is a teaching, as we will see, for which evolution has made us extraordinarily adept learners. From early infancy on, we are taught to obey because "the school, the family, the workplace, the church or synagogue, athletics—all of these institutions function, more or less explicitly, on the basis of obedience to authority." The end result is that "the average individual becomes extremely well versed in the act of obedience" (Miller, 1986:223). Given this habituation, no wonder that "the habit of obedience dies hard" (Tiger and Fox, 1971:29).

Among humans, then, obedience springs from diverse sources and it would be manifestly erroneous to attribute all obedience entirely to our evolutionary heritage. We believe, however, that our inherent tendency to submit provides the most powerful, but by no means only, explanation for what Nobel Laureate Herbert Simon (1990:1665) has euphemistically termed "human docility."

OBEDIENCE AS A COROLLARY OF DOMINANCE AND HIERARCHY

Since the relevant central propositions of contemporary neo-Darwinism have already been presented in the preceding sections, the discussion here can be quite brief.

Dominance relations evolve in a social species such as ours because they optimize the inclusive fitness of the individuals who constitute that species. Dominance relations lead to hierarchical social structures. Hierarchy of itself, though, is not sufficient. If these structures are to reduce intraspecific violence (and so optimize the inclusive fitness of both dominants and subordinates)

there must also concurrently evolve, in Eibl-Eibesfeldt's phrase, "a disposition to accept subordination and obedience" (1989:309). In short, however
repugnant the idea, natural selection has endowed us with "a readiness to
comply with a submissive role" (van der Molen, 1990:63) or, as Barash
would have it, with "an inclination to follow orders, an appropriate behavior
for a species organized along distinct lines of dominance" (1979:186).

Acts of obedience are of two sorts. In one, the organism does something
that it would prefer not to do; in the other, the organism refrains from doing
something that, left to its own choices, it would prefer to do. An example of
the former would be a situation in which a subordinate chimpanzee gives
up a desirable resting place to a dominant; in the latter, it refrains from
copulating with a receptive female because of the threat, explicit or implicit,
of a dominant.

In the case of chimpanzees—or members of any other social species—
obedience is rendered to a more dominant fellow conspecific, that is, one
who occupies a superior place in the group's social hierarchy. Humans, to
be sure, live in many hierarchies. In this discussion, though, we are concerned only with political obedience, that is, actions taken by subordinates
in response to the commands, again implicit or explicit, of those above them
in the political (or sometimes military) hierarchy. So long as that hierarchy
is perceived as "legitimate,"[2] our genetic tendency is to obey. As Kelman
and Hamilton stress, one "striking phenomenon of hierarchies of authority . . . is the readiness of citizens to accept orders unquestioningly . . . even
when obedience entails enormous personal sacrifices or the commitment of
actions that, under other circumstances, they would consider morally rep-
rehensible" (1989:137).

Obedience is thus a behavioral correlate of dominance and hierarchy. If
inclusive fitness is to be optimized, a social species must evolve all three
behaviors—dominance relations, hierarchical social systems, and obedience. All three, surely, are characteristic of Homo sapiens. Not surprisingly,
this disposition or inclination can be discerned at a very youthful age:
according to Stayton, Hogan, and Ainsworth, the "earliest manifestation of
obedience in an infant appears in the final first quarter of the first year of
life" (1971:1058). Discussing similar results achieved with slightly older
children, they comment that:

These findings cannot be predicted from models of socialization which assume that
special intervention is necessary to modify otherwise asocial tendencies of children.
Clearly, these findings require a theory that assumes that an infant is initially
inclined to be social and [somewhat later] ready to obey those persons who are most
significant in his social environment. (1971:1058)

It is possible, of course, to agree that humans consistently manifest these behaviors and yet to deny that the behaviors have a genetic basis. This view is sometimes encountered even within the neo-Darwinian camp among those who accept evolutionary theory as it applies to all other species but nonetheless are convinced that "human beings in their social behavior, alone, have succeeded in escaping biology" (Degler, 1991:viii). Such a position is logically tenable if one believes that there is a vast, unbridgeable gap between all other forms of life, including the great apes, and ourselves.

However, the contention that biology cannot and does not provide an acceptable explanation for human behavior is more commonly encountered among those who see that behavior is primarily, if not totally, determined by "learning." This, in fact, was the overwhelmingly prevailing wisdom in American social and behavioral sciences until at least the 1950s[3] and, though now gradually losing adherents, it probably remains the majority position today.

With regard to obedience, then, psychologists, social psychologists, and other behavioral scientists who are psychologically oriented almost invariably explain both history and experimental results involving obedience in terms of learning and socialization[4] rather than as having some genetic basis.[5] Ralf Dahrendorf, one of Europe's preeminent social scientists, captured both the essence of this belief and, quite unintentionally, the underlying emotional dynamics—when he voiced the "quasi-consolation that our body is not the 'real' us, [and] that biological concepts and theories cannot affect the integrity of our individuality" (1968:20).

Since nothing is to be gained by rehashing here the "nature versus nurture"[6] dispute, two questions must suffice as counterarguments. First, does not the near universality of obedience point to an underlying "human nature" as a major, though not necessarily exclusive, operative influence? Second, if obedience is simply learned, how other than in terms of genetic preprogramming can we explain the remarkable readiness of Homo sapiens to acquire and exhibit this behavior across the ages and around the world?

THE CASE FROM HISTORY

> Nothing has ever been more insupportable for a man and a human
> society than freedom.
>   Fyodor Dostoyevsky, *The Brothers Karamazov*, 1957

The historical evidence for our species' willingness to obey those in authority is so overwhelming and unambiguous that it hardly requires extended discussion.

It might be useful to begin by distinguishing between what appear to be two types of obedience. First, there is the obedience displayed in sanctioned massacres, of which the most recent instances (at the time of this writing) were the mass slaughters in Rwanda and Bosnia. Understandably, the popular media, as well as behavioral scientists (and historians), are prone to focus on these horrifying events when discussing obedience. But, second, sanctioned massacres are better understood, we think, as an extreme manifestation of a far more common human behavior—humankind's customary obedience to the commands of established political authority. We will look briefly at both types.

Sanctioned Massacres

Sanctioned massacres are those in which mass slaughters, often accompanied by torture, mayhem, and rape, are committed in obedience to the commands, implicit or explicit, of established political (or military) authority. Regrettably, even if we limit our survey to the past century or so, all too many examples come to mind. A greatly shortened list would include the Holocaust, My Lai, Katyn, the extermination of the kulaks and the great purges in the USSR, and wholesale authorized killings in Armenia, Indonesia, Cambodia, Rwanda, and Bosnia.[7]

Conceivably, the term might be stretched to subsume also those instances where the command is to commit mass suicide rather than to kill others. If so, we would add to the grim list such tragedies as Massada in Roman times and, in our own day, Jonestown (where perhaps 800 persons took poison) and Waco.

For many, the most profoundly disturbing aspect of sanctioned massacres (the frightful suffering and loss of life aside) is that they are usually carried out not by psychotics or even specially hardened personnel, but by individuals very much like ourselves. Passionately as we would prefer to believe otherwise, it is indisputable that "under orders from an authority . . . many normal people respond with obedience, despite their own scruples and discomfort about actions that they and others would usually regard as illegal, immoral, *and even unthinkable*" (Kelman and Hamilton, 1989:23; italics added). Nor does there seem to be any notable difference in acquiescence by rank and bureaucratic position and thus, presumably, by social position and educational background. As Kelman and Hamilton further remark (1989:23), "The degree of unquestioning obedience to orders shown by officers and functionaries at high levels of the organizational hierarchy is often striking."

At first glance, the "inhuman" behaviors exhibited in authorized massacres seem to be of a totally different order from anything with which we are familiar. That perception is probably misleading. Authorized massacres, most of those who have studied the phenomenon concur, can be better and more productively understood as differing quantitatively rather than qualitatively from the obedience that characterizes so much of "normal" political life. It is to this second type that we now turn.

General Political Obedience

If we were to view some 6,000 years of recorded political society as a landscape in time, there would stretch out before us a vast, desolate desert of absolutism, tyranny,[8] and authoritarianism, only rarely relieved by an oasis of relative freedom and democracy. To be sure, no two governments are quite the same; still, aside from a small handful, states have differed from each other primarily in the degree of obedience and service demanded from their subjects. Laura Betzig (1986) has described in gruesome detail the often almost unbelievable acts of subservience, submission, and sacrifice compelled by rulers of what we might call "primitive" political societies. In that respect, the record of more "advanced" polities, from Babylonia and ancient Egypt to the present, is sometimes only marginally better.[9]

For six millennia or more, rulers have commanded—and almost always their subjects have obeyed. Major collective acts of rebellion have been so relatively infrequent that almost any reasonably well educated person is familiar with most of them. Furthermore, in many instances these revolts against established authority spring from an attempt by a subject peoples to cast off foreign rule or, more precisely, that perceived as foreign. When looking at these essentially colonial uprisings, two points should be kept in mind: First, and this has been especially true the past century or so, many of these rebellions might not have occurred, and almost certainly would not have been successful, were it not for external encouragement and assistance. Second, whatever the justifying rhetoric, these were actually struggles for national and ethnic independence rather than for equality and democracy. In most, though happily not all instances, the native regimes that succeeded the ousted foreign rulers were just as undemocratic as their predecessors.

Any objective reading of history, we submit, permits only one conclusion. From the origin of organized political society, and over sixty some centuries of authoritarian and tyrannical rule by native and alien governors alike, the nearly (but fortunately not completely) invariable human response has been to obey.[10] Taken in broad historical perspective, disobedience is a rarely encountered political phenomenon.

THE EXPERIMENTAL EVIDENCE

The Milgram Experiments

Arguably, the most famous (or infamous, depending upon one's view-point) research on "obedience to authority" were the experiments conducted by Stanley Milgram between 1960 and 1963. Since almost anyone likely to read this book is probably already familiar with his work, it needs to be discussed only briefly here.

What will "normal" people do, Milgram (1974) sought to ascertain, when ordered to impose electric shocks, of increasing severity (and painfulness), on another person?[11] Forty men, representing a variety of professions, were recruited as subjects via mail and newspaper solicitation. These forty were instructed to play the role of teachers in the experimental situation; members of Milgram's team played the ostensible role of learners.

Each teacher was told to read a series of word pairs to the learner and then to read the first word of a pair and four possible associations. The learners were to indicate which of the four associations had in fact been paired with the first. The instructions authorized the teacher to punish the learner for each error of recall by pressing a lever on a shock generator.

The shock generator operated by the teacher had a panel with thirty levers; the levers (the teachers were informed) administered electrical shocks to the learners in strengths ranging from 15 to 450 volts, as indicated on each lever. So that there would be no ambiguity as to the strength of the shock, many of the levers also had an additional marking, starting with "Slight Shock" and going to "Very Strong Shock," "Intense Shock," "Extreme Intensity Shock," and finally "Danger: Severe Shock." These last two levers were further marked "XXX." As the experiment was designed, the teachers could also hear (but not see) the learners (presumably) pounding on the wall in pain as the shock level (presumably) increased and became progressively more painful.

In those instances where the teacher seemed reluctant to administer a shock, the experimenter would respond with one of four prods of increasing urgency: (1) "Please continue" or "please go on," (2) "The experiment requires that you continue," (3) "It is absolutely essential that you continue," and (4) "You have no other choice, you must go on."

The results? Contrary to the expectations of three groups (including thirty-nine psychiatrists) asked to predict the probable behaviors, and to Milgram's surprise and dismay, 26 of the 40 subjects obeyed when, in the course of the experiment, they were ordered to press the 450-volt ("XXX Danger: Extreme Intensity Shock") lever. True, some of them hesitated;

many, according to Milgram, "were observed to sweat, tremble, stutter, bite their lips, groan, and dig their fingernails into their flesh" (1974:375). Many hesitated, many seemed disturbed—but they obeyed.

Milgram himself was appalled by the outcome of his experiment. The "chief finding" and "the fact most urgently demanding explanation," he wrote, ". . . is the extreme willingness of adults to go to almost any lengths on the command of an authority" (1974:14). How, then, to explain this willingness to obey?

The subjects obeyed, in his opinion, because "we are born with a *potential* for obedience, which then interacts with the influence of society to produce the obedient man." In this sense, the capacity for obedience is like the capacity for language: "certain highly specific mental structures must be present" (1974:125). That innate capacity for obedience, Milgram ruefully concluded, "is the fatal flaw that nature has designed into us, and which in the long run gives our species only a modest chance of survival" (1974:188).

Many social scientists, needless to say, refused to accept Milgram's results as valid;[12] others, while not challenging his results, found other explanations more persuasive.[13] The latter issue remains a matter of controversy; his results, though, have been repeatedly replicated.

Other Experimental Inquiries into Obedience

Milgram was not the first psychologist to explore conformity to command and social pressure. Jerome Frank (1944) had previously demonstrated that an experimenter could lead subjects to consume a nauseating quantity of soda crackers. Earlier, Muzafer Sherif (1936) had shown that judgments (regarding a point of light in a darkened laboratory) were readily swayed by the (apparently differing) opinions of others. And, of course, Solomon Asch, for whom Milgram had once served as an assistant, presented convincing evidence (1956) that peer pressure could lead the subjects to make "glaring errors on an unambiguous line-estimation problem" (Miller, 1986:16).

As might be expected, Milgram's work not only provoked a torrent of discussion but also inspired many attempts to replicate—or possibly contradict—his findings.[14] David Mantell (1971) essentially duplicated Milgram's experiment, requiring the subjects to administer electrical shocks, and so forth. Although Mantell later described the laboratory setting in which the subjects performed as "senseless," the subjects nonetheless obeyed.

Changing the research design to provide a nonhuman "victim," Sheridan and King (1972) instructed their subjects, as part of a putative study of canine visual discrimination, to shock a "cute, fluffy puppy." More than half of the male subjects and, curiously enough, 100 percent of the female subjects, were "maximally obedient." Kilham and Mann (1974) further varied the experiment by having their subjects transmit to someone else, rather than personally execute, the orders to shock the (in this instance, a human) "learner." Again, the prevailing response was obedience—even up to the fictitious 450-volt level. And, in a recent Dutch version of the Milgram format, the overwhelming majority of subjects complied as instructed (Meeus and Raaijmakers, 1985).

Obedience experimentation has not been limited to adults. Slightly modifying Milgram's paradigm, Shanab and Yahya (1978) tested the willingness of Jordanian public school students to follow commands. Almost three-quarters of those involved obeyed up to and including the highest shock level. Much the same results were achieved, they found, when essentially the same experiment was undertaken with college students (1978).

An interesting modification was introduced by John Martin and his associates. There, the subjects—13- and 14-year-old male schoolchildren—were ordered to carry out tasks (listening to sounds at increasingly high frequencies) that were "clearly and explicitly described as potentially harmful to themselves" (1976:346). Some 95 percent turned the dial to the level that, they had been told, carried with it the danger of a 20 percent possibility of hearing loss; over half of them then went on to the maximum level.

These studies constitute a fairly representative, albeit by no means complete, list of the obedience experiments undertaken to date.[15] There is no need to belabor the point: however the experiments differed in detail and design, the results were almost always the same—the subjects obeyed.

DISCUSSION

As previously emphasized, there undoubtedly are a number of reasons for this demonstrated human readiness to comply with even absurd commands. Interestingly enough, even so radical a thinker as Auguste Comte agreed, writing that "there is a much stronger inclination to obedience in the generality of men than it is customary in our day to suppose" (cited by Chambliss, 1954:413).[16]

Few friends of democracy are as yet prepared to accept, and fewer still will welcome, that judgment—not even from Hegel and Comte united. Nonetheless, it is consistent with and supported by the overwhelming weight of historical and experimental evidence. Furthermore, however initially distasteful to democratic sensibilities, it opens the way to a more realistic understanding of actual political behavior. Perhaps most important of all, the assertion provides, as we will subsequently propose, a possible point of departure for a democratic public policy aimed at influencing that behavior.

NOTES

1. Strictly speaking, evolutionary theory does not provide evidence of obedience but, rather, a conceptual framework for explaining human history, on the one hand, and laboratory findings, on the other.

2. Essentially paraphrasing Easton (1965), a government (or regime or political community) is "legitimate" when a population believes that, on balance, it meets its needs and interests and reflects its cultural and/or ethnic identity. When governments (regimes, etc.) are no longer perceived as legitimate, they can still extract obedience by force and threat, but in most instances their days are numbered.

3. For a masterful overview of the rise, decline, and subsequent resurrection of Darwinism as applied to human behavior, see Carl Degler's *In Search of Human Nature* (1991).

4. See, for example, Ervin Staub, *The Roots of Evil* (1989), and Herman C. Kelman and V. Lee Hamilton, *Crimes of Obedience* (1989). Barrington Moore's *Injustice: The Social Bases of Obedience and Revolt* (1978) is curiously ambivalent. Moore agrees that "moral codes, moral anger, and hence a sense of social injustice may have some very important roots in human biology" (p. 7) but apparently does not recognize the possibility that obedience may also have a biological basis.

5. Freudians who have dealt with obedience, for instance, Eric Fromm in his *Escape from Freedom* (1941), constitute an obvious exception. But Freudian theorists, and certainly the master himself, take an essentially biological view of the mainsprings of human behavior.

6. A key element in neo-Darwinian thought, we should add, is that this is a false dichotomy and that the two are nigh inseparable in the actual development of an organism's behavior.

7. Harff and Gurr (1995:26–27) identify almost fifty separate instances of "genocides and politicides" that have occurred since World War II.

8. "For most of recorded history, the tyrannical use of power has been only too common" (Chirot, 1994:5).

9. Arguing that, whatever the mode of governance, "overall human suffering remains the same," Vivek Patkar suggests that "a principle of the conservation of human suffering is in operation in some form" (1993:1).

10. The weight of the evidence would surely seem to support the bleak judgement of Dostoyevsky's Grand Inquisitor that "nothing has ever been more insupportable for a man and a human society than freedom" (1957:233).

11. We have relied heavily for a description of the Milgram experiments upon Miller (1986) and Kelman and Hamilton (1989).

12. Here again, we are indebted to Miller (1986), who provides a detailed description and analysis of both the criticisms and the replicative experiments generated by Milgram's studies.

13. Kelman and Hamilton, for instance, argue that "it is more instructive to look . . . at the conditions under which the usual moral inhibitions against violence become weakened" (1989:15).

14. Apparently unaware of Milgram's work, C. K. Hofling and his colleagues (1966) conducted a "real life" experiment in which nurses in a hospital were instructed by a "physician" to administer a certain drug to one of their patients. The instructions violated several hospital regulations—and the "physician" issuing the instruction (via phone) was not known to the nurse. Of 22 nurses so ordered, 21 were prepared to obey.

Rank and Jacobson (1977) achieved quite different results in a somewhat similar inquiry but, as Miller (1986:85–86) points out, there were important structural differences between the two studies.

15. We should mention, though, the less academic but no less telling experiment on obedience and conformity conducted by Allan Funt of *Candid Camera* fame:

In one instance, Funt placed his telephone number in a help-wanted advertisement, then arranged personal interviews with those who responded. We are shown an interviewee as he is directed to a small office in which several other persons are already seated, apparently waiting. To the experimental subject, the others appear to be fellow interviewees, but we know they are really confederates of Mr. Funt. Responding to no apparent signal, the others abruptly rise from their seats and begin taking off their clothing. We are shown a close-up of the experimental subject, his face a mask of apprehension as he surveys what is happening. A few moments pass, then he, too, rises from his chair and proceeds to disrobe. At no point during this process does he ask any of the others why they are removing their clothing. As the scene ends, we see him standing there, naked alongside the others, apparently waiting for some clue as to what happens next. (Frank, 1985:18)

16. Carlyle and Nietzsche immediately come to mind as other nineteenth-century philosophers who shared this conviction.

Chapter 7

Indoctrinability

THE BIOLOGICAL BASIS OF BELIEF

Homo sapiens display, we have argued, the genetically transmitted pro-clivities for dominance, hierarchy, and obedience that also characterize the other social primates. Our species has also evolved, however, a behavioral trait that is unarguably unique among living creatures. We refer, of course, to the capacity to accept and then to act on the basis of beliefs and values—even when the resulting actions run counter to our innate inclinations or our personal desires. As one of our most eminent biologists put it, "of all living creatures, human beings are uniquely capable of disobeying those biological inclinations that whisper within them. We alone are able to say 'No' to such genetic tendencies as may predispose some of us to polygyny, theft, murder, etc." (Barash, 1994:16). It is this truly remarkable trait that is denoted by the admittedly awkward and cumbersome term, "indoctrinability."[1]

Because of indoctrinability, ideas, values, and beliefs can profoundly alter the behaviors of those who embrace them. In a sense, to follow up our earlier discussion, we become obedient to ideas and ideals. Or, to put the matter in a more epigrammatic form, "Humans have become intrinsically different from apes by becoming, in a very limited but real sense, artifacts of their own artifacts" (Kingdon, 1993:3).

When this occurs, as it so often does, culture triumphs over nature, even over some of our most basic drives.[2] To offer a few examples out of the many that come almost immediately to mind:

1. The practice of celibacy among Roman Catholic priests demonstrates that religious conviction can override the most demanding drive of all living beings—sex and reproduction.

2. From Thermopylae to the present, endless millions of men and women have died in behalf of cherished ethnic, religious, and nationalistic beliefs, as indoctrinability has triumphed over the individual desire for survival.

3. From Massada to Jonestown, humankind has engaged in episodes of collective suicide in behalf of some cause or value. This is perhaps indoctrinability carried to its ultimate end.

Heroic or classic examples are hardly needed. All of us can think of numerous instances in which, faced with difficult choices, we either did not do something that we very much wanted to do or did something that we would have greatly preferred not doing. These omissions or actions were taken in obedience to the moral imperatives that we call "conscience." Die-hard Platonists aside, very few people think that we were born with these moral dictates already firmly implanted in our minds, waiting only to be revealed. These concepts of right and wrong were acquired, rather, from our environment and our life experiences. The ability to acquire them, and their ability, as our conscience, to influence our actions, is a familiar, possibly all too familiar, aspect of indoctrinability.[3] All of us have made sacrifices, too, often very substantial sacrifices, in behalf of some deeply felt belief system, whether social, religious, or political. The capacity to hold abstract values, and their reciprocal ability frequently to dictate our actions, are simply further aspects of indoctrinability. In short, whether manifested in the form of conscience or of ideational commitment, indoctrinability is demonstrably capable of inducing behaviors that run counter to our own desires and, on occasion, to our genetic inclinations.

To be sure, given the basic bias of our evolutionary inheritance, humans are predisposed to embrace authoritarian political, social,[4] and even religious[5] beliefs. Until the early 1800s, the history of political philosophy shows (see chapter 8), philosophical and popular opinion alike strongly favored authoritarian and decried democratic political doctrines. In helping to reinforce our hierarchical bias, indoctrinability has probably contributed significantly to the predominance and persistence of authoritarian governance throughout human history.

But the capacity to believe and then to act on the basis of those beliefs is not limited to any specific set of ideas. There is almost no limit to the range and variety, or eccentricity, of the values humans are capable of accepting and acting upon. This is true in religion, in philosophy, in ethics, in art—and in politics. By its very nature, consequently, indoctrinability carries with it a potential susceptibility to democratic notions, however we might be otherwise genetically inclined. It is this potentiality that, when combined with the requisite confluence of economic and social conditions previously discussed, enables democratic ideas to take hold, to influence political behavior, and thus to make democracy sometimes possible.

Indoctrinability, then, together with dominance, hierarchy, and obedience, is one of the innate behavioral capacities and characteristics of our species. As might be expected, in most instances indoctrinability serves to support and reinforce these generally authoritarian tendencies. Under other and fairly special conditions, though, indoctrinability provides a window of opportunity for the acceptance of democratic ideas and of political actions that, if successful, lead to the establishment of a democratic polity.

We should keep in mind, though, that democratic polities, no matter how impressive or apparently firmly seated, run counter to our social primate nature. Indoctrinabilty, in conjunction with the requisite material conditions, may make democracy feasible. But unless both of these requirements are satisfied and perpetuated (a problem we address in our next chapter), the mode of governance will revert, sooner or later, to a type more closely reflecting the inherent preferences of that underlying nature.

EVOLUTIONARY ORIGINS

Indoctrinability, like dominance, hierarchy, and obedience, is an evolved behavior. To have evolved, it must have served an evolutionary function,[6] just as did these other behavioral patterns. That is, it must have contributed to the inclusive fitness of the individual and/or to the fitness of the group, an idea that has once again become acceptable to some neo-Darwinian theorists such as David Sloan Wilson (1995). The evolutionary how and why of indoctrinability is thus the subject of the balance of this chapter.

Indoctrinability and Individual-Level Selection

From a neo-Darwinian perspective, individual selection for indoctrinability in a language-capable species makes sound evolutionary sense. When individuals accept the same values, conflict and violence will be diminished, resulting in a more stable society.[7] From the vantage point of the conforming individual, relative order and tranquility, in turn, are likely to result in greater reproductive success and, hence, inclusive fitness. As Edward O. Wilson has observed (1978:187):

The ability of individuals to conform permits them to enjoy the benefits of membership with a minimum of energy expenditure and risk, and their behavior is sustained over long periods of time as the norm. Although the rivals of the conformists in the society may gain momentary advantage through selfishness and irreverence, it is lost in the long term through ostracism and repression.

Thus, individuals' indoctrinability creates the conditions for a more stable society, which itself enhances the odds of reproductive success.

Indoctrinability and Group-Level Selection

Group selection has often been viewed as a bête noire by evolutionary theorists (e.g., Dawkins, 1989b; Williams, 1966). However, even leading sociobiologists have conceded that group selection can occur under certain circumstances (e.g., Wilson, 1975).

Group selection, simply, is the process of natural selection operating at the level of the group or society. While the concept remains contentious, a number of eminent evolutionary theorists do believe that under specified conditions, selection can operate at the group level (e.g., Gould, 1992; Wilson and Sober, 1994). Brandon has summarized when we might see group selection take place (1988:58):

In summary, group selection occurs if and only if (1) there is differential reproduction of groups and (2) . . . [d]ifferential group reproduction is best explained in terms of differences in group-level properties (differences in group adaptedness to a common selective environment).

While Brandon offers this as a hypothesis to be tested, it provides a useful starting point for us.

Simply, if we have a variety of human groups living in a similar environment and indoctrinability characterizes some groups and not others, we may see a process beginning that goes like this. If those groups whose members are more apt to be indoctrinable produce more viable offspring—and there is a genetic basis to the tendency to indoctrinate—then selection for indoctrinability could take place at the group level.

Given the controversy surrounding the idea, we do not press it here. However, this is a theoretical possibility that should at least be raised.

Indoctrinability as Side Effect: An Alternative Hypothesis

Before proceeding, though, we should consider an alternative proposition, that is, that indoctrinability did not evolve because it served an important inclusive fitness function but, rather, that it is a side effect of genes related to behaviors that do play such a role. That indoctrinability is merely the quirky by-product of selection for other behavior(s) seems quite unlikely. It too nicely complements and reinforces obedience, dominance, and hierarchy to be an accidental outcome, we believe. Furthermore, a good case can be made, as we have just outlined, that indoctrinability importantly enhances the inclusive fitness of the individual (and of the group as well). This would argue that it has been selected for itself, rather than being what economists would term a "free rider."

On the other hand, there is certainly a very close relationship between indoctrinability and one other attribute that also seems to be almost equally unique to humans. That attribute, of course, is language.[8] Conceivably, indoctrinability—or a latent capacity for it—antedated language; more probably, it evolved either concurrently with language or slightly thereafter.

Indoctrinability and Self-Deception

The case for indoctrinability as a factor that might make democracy's continuation possible, thus laid out, seems reasonable. However, another impulse among humans is associated with this as well—the tendency to deceive ourselves. Humans appear to have the remarkable propensity to allow themselves to be deceived. This is a corollary, of course, to indoctrinability. We come to accept certain beliefs, such as the desire for democracy, and then deceive ourselves that this is the only possible way properly to organize government affairs. In this manner, we contribute to social stability by becoming unable to comprehend other ways of doing things. Alexander argues that natural selection can operate so that "the self-deceiver does not (necessarily) know he is deceiving himself" (Alexander, 1987:123).

Mechanisms for self-deception can include psychological processes such as rationalization, reaction formation, repression of memories, projecting unacceptable attitudes onto others, and so on (e.g., see Lockard, 1980:260). Interestingly, authoritarians tend to carry out less self-deception than nonauthoritarian people (Lockard, 1980:267–268). Thus, people believing in democracy may be more susceptible to self-deception![9]

Robert Wright notes the end result of this process (1994:324–325):

We believe the things—about morality, personal worth, even objective truth—that lead to behaviors that get our genes into the next generation. . . . It is the behavioral goals—status, sex, effective coalition, parental investment, and so on—that remain steadfast while our view of reality adjusts to accommodate that constancy. What is in our genes' interests is what seems "right"—morally right, objectively right, whatever sort of rightness is in order.

Including, one might add, the rightness of democracy as the best form of government.

If people come to believe in this, society becomes more stable, enhancing the odds of reproductive success. And if people self-deceive to take democracy as the best form of government as a given, then stability is all the greater. People seldom challenge that which is obvious and commonsense. Thus, if we become indoctrinated to democratic values and then self-deceive that this is obviously the right and proper form of government, stability is more likely to take place.[10]

DISCUSSION

Therefore, a persuasive case can be made that indoctrinability, just as did the capacity for language, served on balance to enhance the inclusive fitness of the individual and possibly served to enhance group survival. Still, in evolution as elsewhere, there are few benefits without a price. Originally, it seems safe to say, indoctrinability served to lessen discord (and ultimately violence) in relatively small societies of social primates, with consequent benefits to both individuals and the collective group. But as the size and complexity of the groups increased from hunting-gathering bands of perhaps thirty to forty persons to nation-states numbering millions and hundreds of millions, and as rival interests and ideas began increasingly to compete with each other, indoctrinability has become a fecund source both of intrasocietal ethnic and religious[11] violence and of inter-state hostility, bloodshed, and warfare. Indoctrinability evolved to meet the needs of a totally different environment; accordingly, Barash has aptly described its often biologically dysfunctional consequences in today's world as an "artificial exaggeration of an otherwise adaptive tendency" (Barash, 1994:15).

Different groups within diverse societies can come to live in distinct worlds, fiercely adhering to their varying views of reality. They can become indoctrinated into competing value systems, and this may trigger furious internal strife, as the breakup of Yugoslavia amply illustrates.

In this respect, indoctrinability has had social consequences often profoundly different from those of its fellow evolved behaviors—dominance, hierarchy, and obedience. On balance, the latter tend, for better or worse, to hold societies together. Indoctrinability, though, is Janus-faced or, if another simile is preferred, either Dr. Jekyll or Mr. Hyde. Depending upon the circumstances, it can bind—or it can serve as a profoundly disruptive force. It is this latter capacity that makes it possible for democratic movements to emerge and even sometimes to replace the authoritarian modes of govern-ance that have been the historical norm for our species.

Democratic political movements, though, require special social and economic enabling conditions if they are to be successful. No less important, these special enabling conditions (or their equivalents) must be protected and perpetuated if democratic government, given our species' inherent social primate hierarchical bias, is, in Lincoln's words, to "long endure." And that is the problem that we address in the concluding chapter of this book.

NOTES

1. For classic discussions, one could consult Fromm (1941) or Rokeach (1960). For excellent bibliographies, see Shinn (1987) and, more recently, Salter (1995).

2. The victory may be relatively short-lived or of surprising duration.

3. The evolution of conscience and of morality has generated a considerable literature. On this see Alexander (1987) and, more recently, Wright (1994).

4. Think of the frequency with which children's fairy tales are peopled by and center on the behaviors of princes and princesses, kings and queens, the good and the evil alike.

5. Consider how Islam, Christianity, and Judaism are based on the presumed teachings of a single person or the special authority widely (if not universally) conceded to the mullahs, priests, clergy, and rabbis.

6. We use the past tense here not because indoctrinability has necessarily lost that function but because, with the invention of nuclear weaponry, it could lead to actions that might wipe out the species itself. In a very literal sense, we are an endangered species—with the danger of extinction arising from our fellow con-specifics. For this reason, no doubt, Barash (1994:15) has spoken of indoctrinabil-ity as "an artificial exaggeration of an otherwise adaptive tendency."

7. See, for example, Eibl-Eibesfeldt, "Warfare, Man's Indoctrinability, and Group Selection," *Zeitschrift für Tierpsychologie* 60 (1982):177–198.

8. There are those, to be sure, who insist that other species (chimpanzees, perhaps dolphins) may also have a capacity for language, as that term is normally understood.

9. If our logic is correct and authoritarianism is more compatible with human nature, this makes a certain amount of sense. Self-deception is less important for someone doing things that are relatively natural; self-deception becomes more salient to maintain the behavior of people who are acting in a way less natural to their biological impulses.

10. Democracy is underlain by a very optimistic view of humans' ability to govern themselves wisely (or at least adequately). This optimism may have an

evolutionary basis, as Lionel Tiger points out (Tiger, 1979). And this optimism
itself is often a form of self-deception.

11. "Men never do evil so completely and cheerfully as when they do it from
religious conviction" (Pascal, *Pensées*, 1670).

Chapter 8

Democratic Philosophy: From Ugly Duckling to Irresistible Swan

INTRODUCTION

If evolution has endowed our species with a bias toward rule by a relative few, it would be reasonable to expect that bias to be reflected in both the writings of our political philosophers and in the political preferences of the population at large. It was.

From Grecian times to the present, democracy has been a near pariah among our greatest and most influential political philosophers; as neo-Darwinian theory would predict, it was also widely held in popular disrepute until at least the early 1800s. These negative philosophical and public views of democracy constitute the first subject to be addressed in this chapter.

Since the midnineteenth century, though, there has been a seemingly profound reversal of public attitudes toward democracy, a change which, gathering momentum in the twentieth century, has made democracy the most widely used political catchword of our age. Surveying the contemporary scene, Robert Dahl was certainly correct in concluding that "today, the idea of democracy is universally popular" (1989:2).[1] How, given our basic thesis, can we explain this apparently contradictory development?

Two factors were operative—one general, the other more specifically related to democratic ideology. The former springs from our species' afore-mentioned capacity to create values and then to act in pursuance of these values even when these values and actions run counter to our genetic inclinations. Given this extraordinary human trait, democracy might conceivably have achieved some popular acceptance, at least among some groups, despite our innate authoritarian inclinations.

But a second factor, the originally and then increasingly ambiguous nature of democratic theory, greatly facilitated a far wider acceptance. That ambiguity, consequently, constitutes the second major theme of this chapter, because much of democracy's present-day popularity stems from the fact that the term actually subsumes two quite different—and ultimately contradictory[2]—concepts. One of these is the idea of "inalienable human rights"; the other, of course, is the notion of political equality as embodied in universal suffrage. (Not surprisingly, the former gained acceptance much earlier than did the latter.) In political reality, these two ideals are almost inevitably bound to clash; but when joined together, despite their inherent logical incompatibility, they immeasurably enhance the attractiveness of democratic doctrine.

The increasingly common tendency to use the term to describe and justify efforts to attain independence by subject peoples living under foreign rule added yet another dimension to the already diverse connotations of "democracy." This common-law marriage with nationalistic aspirations undoubtedly contributed further to democracy's mass appeal—and further expanded its already multiple meanings.

Worse confusion was yet to come. In the twentieth century the term experienced its ultimate (or so we can hope) distortion and degradation. Political societies with impeccable totalitarian credentials promptly proceeded to call themselves "people's democracies"; to describe their despotic systems of decision making (and implacable elimination of opposition, real or alleged) as "democratic centralism"; then, for an additional cosmetic touch, even to hold "elections."

In short, a credible case can be made that a major—though certainly not the only—reason for the present popularity of democracy is that the word has been employed to mean whatever the user, emulating the Red Queen, wants it to mean. But, as Dahl has ruefully observed, "a term that means anything means nothing. And so it has become with 'democracy'" (1989:2).

Now, to explore these two aforementioned themes. The first, to repeat, is that there has been a long-standing philosophical and, until quite recently, popular antipathy to democratic ideas. The second is that the present widespread popularity of democracy derives, in substantial measure, from the original ambiguity of the concept and its subsequent further loss of specific substantive content over the past century or so.

DEMOCRACY ON DEARTH: UNLOVED AND UNWANTED

To begin, we will utilize—with great originality—the device of a fictitious journey to a distant planet. After speedily mastering the local language, we learn the following:

The inhabitants call their planet "Dearth." We have arrived on Dearth at a time that corresponds roughly to our own world's late seventeenth or early eighteenth century (C.E.). The recorded history of Dearth extends about 6,000 years or so into the past. During these half-dozen millennia, many hundreds of political states—some small, some truly empires—have come and gone. Of these, only two were what earthlings would call democracies, and both were quite short-lived. All the other polities in Dearth's history were authoritarian—that is, based on the dominion of the few over the many—and differed from each other primarily to the extent that some were more authoritarian, some less.

We also learn that while Dearth has had many famous political philosophers, not a single one of them supported the idea of democratic government. Over the past few decades, though, a few of Dearth's most liberal thinkers have expressed the belief that all Dearthians were endowed by nature with certain basic and inalienable rights. On the other hand, all of Dearth's leading political theorists (including the aforementioned "liberals") have been united in their opposition—they disagreed only in the degree of their distaste—to the idea that government should rest on, and act in accordance with, the will of the numerical majority.

So much for Dearth's most eminent political theorists. How did the general population, that is, the citizenry at large, feel about democracy? Dearth's philosophers, we discover, reflected as well as shaped popular views on this matter. Insofar as the available evidence indicates, the rank-and-file Dearthian (like their intellectual betters) regarded the notion of political rule by the many as manifestly, even absurdly, contrary to the natural and proper order of things.

The nearly total absence of democratic governments in Dearth's history, the unanimous opposition to democratic theories among Dearth's leading philosophers, and the manifest popular aversion to the idea of rule by the majority suggest the operation of some powerful underlying attitudinal bias. Was it possible that the Dearthians' evolutionary past had somehow inclined them to favor authoritarian government and to be receptive to authoritarian, and hostile to democratic, political ideas? And if so. . . .

BACK TO EARTH: THE GREAT PHILOSOPHERS

Dearth, of course, is a transparent and not overly subtle simulacrum for our own planet. Our great philosophers, just like their fictitious Dearthian counterparts, have been unanimous in their hostility to democracy. The point warrants repetition: from Athenian days to the present, no major Western philosopher has endorsed the proposition that public policy should be decided either by direct popular vote or by representatives chosen on the basis of anything approximating universal suffrage. Pericles, to be sure, eulogized Athenian democracy,[3] but Plato's and Aristotle's assessment of rule by the majority ranged from the disparaging to the acutely hostile. Nor did their fellow Greek philosophers disagree.[4]

Neither did the Roman or medieval political theorists who followed. In fact, after the fall of Athens, "for more than 2,000 years nearly all leading minds . . . rejected [the idea of] popular government" (Beer, 1986:391). Not until the English Levellers (John Lilburne, Richard Overton, and Thomas Rainsborough, hardly major intellectual figures), circa 1640, will we find an attempt to justify government resting on the will of the many.

There were, to be sure, prominent advocates of representative government—beginning, say, with Marsiglio of Padua and William of Occam in the fourteenth century, continuing with Nicolas of Cusa and his fellow Conciliarists, and then, in England, continuing with John Locke and John Stuart Mill. With the exception of Mill, though, representative government was understood by its advocates as a system in which the representatives would be chosen not by a numerical majority but, in Marsiglio's classic phrase, by the "prevailing part [of society], both their number and quality in the community being taken into account." And Mill himself, rightly regarded as the preeminent advocate of representative government, was at best ambivalent about the merits of universal suffrage.

What about Jean-Jacques Rousseau? The most one can say here, given the contradictory nature of much of his work, is that while he may have favored representative government, he did not believe in popular democracy, certainly not as we understand the term.[5]

VOX POPULI

So much for our great political theorists and their lack of enthusiasm, to put it mildly, for democracy. But, to repeat an earlier query, what were the views of the citizenry at large on this issue? Until quite recently, the masses held much the same unfavorable opinion of democracy as did the philosophers.[6] As late as the end of the eighteenth century, a leading historian of political thought wrote, "democracy was not thought well of by most people, and certainly not by most of the educated or ruling classes" (Mayo, 1960:25). Lord Bryce (1921), in fact, puts the turning point a half century later. Tawney (1931:54) concurs in this dating, adding that "even in England, where there were no legal barriers separating different social strata, the conception of a hierarchical social order, based on class domination and class subordination, was a powerful element in the prevalent political thought of the age [i.e., the late eighteenth and early nineteenth centuries]" (1931:122).

This appeared to have been the situation in Europe and, to anticipate a possible objection, even in the United States, where the words "democracy" and "democrat" were "generally used and understood by eighteenth-century Americans as terms of political derogation" (Hanson, 1985:56). That disparaging usage was shared by the Founding Fathers themselves, "who preferred republicanism as a word and a theory of government" (Mayo, 1960:25). Not until the Jacksonian era did "democracy" and "democrat" lose their pejorative overtones and begin to acquire a positive connotation.

After that, the pendulum swung swiftly to the opposite end. Barely a century and a half later, mass attitudes had changed to where, as Sartori (1965) ironically remarked, the term had become so sacred that now almost no one dares openly to say that he is antidemocratic. By then, as previously remarked, even the most despotic governments were unabashedly claiming the title of "people's democracy."

In retrospect, it is clear that the initial attraction of democracy was appreciably enhanced by the inherent ambiguity of democracy, encompassing as it does two quite different (and often clashing) values. Over the ensuing decades, the term came to be employed in still other diverse, and sometimes even contradictory, senses. The resulting loss of specific meaning, we think it fair to say, contributed in substantial measure to its concomitant explosive growth in popularity.

THE DUALITY OF DEMOCRATIC DOCTRINE

Democratic ideology as it originally evolved in the late eighteenth and early nineteenth centuries represented an uneasy union of two quite different philosophical concepts. One is the ideal of political equality, which, when translated into political practice, becomes representative government based on universal suffrage (or something close to it),[7] political equality (one person, one vote), and majority rule. The other key concept is the belief in natural and inalienable human rights, often called "liberalism."[8] Originating in the desire to fix effective limits to the power of the state, liberalism posits the rule of law which, to be meaningful, requires an independent judiciary.

Of the two doctrines, that of individual rights is much the older, claiming Cicero and St. Thomas Aquinas among its philosophical progenitors, and Hooker, Locke, Milton, Montesquieu, and John Stuart Mill[9] among its many later distinguished advocates. The proposition that all "men" are by nature entitled to these basic rights achieved wide acceptance by the eighteenth century and was embodied in such famous political enactments as the English Bill of Rights, the French Declaration of Rights, the American Declaration of Independence, and the first ten amendments to the American Constitution.

On the other hand, the second democratic tenet, the concept of popular sovereignty, has a very meager—almost non-existent—philosophical tradition, was much slower in gaining popular approval, and lagged considerably in achieving implementation. Neither England nor the United States, for example, had general male (white, that is) suffrage until the second half of the nineteenth century; true universal suffrage (female and male) did not come until decades later.

The ideas of popular sovereignty, on the one hand, and of liberalism on the other are also quite different conceptually. In Hanson's incisive phrase, "There was nothing intrinsically democratic about liberalism nor was there anything especially liberal about democracy [i.e., rule by the majority]" (1985:13). Not only are they different, they are fundamentally incompatible.[10] Just as John Stuart Mill feared, and political history has often demonstrated, rule by the majority can pose as serious a threat to human freedom as did the despotic monarchical and oligarchical regimes of previous eras.[11]

The vastly divergent emphases of its two major constituent tenets served, in practice, to enhance democracy's popular appeal. Some, believing the idea of inalienable human rights to be the essence of democratic doctrine, were won over by its liberalistic component; others, no doubt, understood democracy in terms of, and were attracted by, that strand that emphasized majority rule based on widespread suffrage. And some, perhaps not realizing or not troubled by the difference between these two ideals, found both attractive.[12]

DEMOCRATIC THEORY: FROM JANUS-FACED TO HYDRA-HEADED

If democratic theory originally faced in two directions, that was only the beginning. It was soon expanded to subsume yet another meaning, the right of a people to self-government. The French Revolution is usually credited for fanning, if not actually igniting, the nationalistic aspirations that have since played so large a role in both international and domestic politics. Around the world, subject peoples having in common some combination of language, religion, history, and culture, sought to throw off foreign domination. Almost everywhere, the demand arose for greater self-government and then, inevitably, independence.

The practice of democracy requires, almost by definition, self-government. But that does not mean that all nationalistic movements were necessarily democratic either in their original aims or in the eventual end product. Conor Cruise O'Brien maintains, in fact, that "nationalism and democracy are qualitatively different and incommensurable" (1991:29). This may be carrying the argument a bit too far. Still, as has occurred innumerable times, many peoples who were successful in throwing off foreign governance simply replaced it with an equally and sometimes much more repressive indigenous regime. The most aggressively nationalistic states of the twentieth century have often been the most authoritarian; and successful nationalist movements have not been notably generous in granting meaningful self-government to other ethnic minorities residing within their borders.

These painful political realities, though, did not deter nationalists around the world from appropriating the language of democracy and from describing their struggle for self-government as democratic. Nor has the substantial difference between these ideas prevented many in the Western world from regarding almost any—unless patently communist inspired, and not always even then—group seeking political independence as having legitimate democratic aspirations. This confusion between the two objectives explains in part, we think, Woodrow Wilson's insistence upon "self-determination" in redrawing the map of Europe after World War I. Of the new states then created, possibly one was still a democracy a bare decade after the event.

Among present-day political ideologies, almost all students agree, nationalism is perhaps the most powerful: George Kennan has called it "the greatest emotional-political force of the age" (1993); going a step further, Hannah Arendt claims that it has led to "the conquest of the state by the nation" (1966:230). In country after country, democratic political movements often sought to expand their popular following by espousing nationalistic objectives. In parallel fashion, nationalistic movements almost always benefited at home, and often gained invaluable moral and material capital abroad, by professing democratic goals. As this process has gone on over the years, the meaning of "democracy" has been further enlarged—and distorted.[13] That distortion, as often happens with an ideology, has served to broaden its appeal.

The final (or so we would hope) degradation of the democratic doctrine requires only brief discussion. Lenin's contention that a truly revolutionary party should emulate the military ideal, that is, command from above and prompt obedience below, was rejected by most European Marxists and alienated many of Lenin's fellow Russian Communists. Nothing if not flexible in these respects, the Bolsheviks, in moving to seize and then to exercise power, speedily adopted the language, though surely not the substance, of democracy. In the USSR and its satellite states the policy-making process, unchanged in reality from the original top-down concept, was hailed as "democratic centralism"; there were elections in which citizens voted (few dared not to) for representatives, although they had no voice in choosing the candidates; the elected representatives, staffing legislative bodies devoid of authority, dutifully raised their hands and voices to approve and applaud the decisions with which they were presented; the various Soviet-style regimes were described as "people's democracies"; and the party's publicists constantly reminded their own people and the world at large that only the people's democracies were true democracies.

For almost three-quarters of a century, official Marxism used the language of egalitarian democracy to describe and praise a system in which some were immeasurably more equal than others, and employed the language of liberalism to hail a political order in which human rights vis-à-vis the state existed neither in theory nor in practice. It became a crime, often a capital offense, to say, to think of saying, or just to be suspected of thinking of saying that Soviet society was in any way not completely democratic.

For decades, the charade was remarkably successful. Within the communist states, many found it possible to believe the party line. Outside the Soviet sphere, and especially in the Third World, millions of people, having no idea of the reality, accepted Stalinism at its own word. Even where better information was readily available, as in the United States and Western Europe, many simply denied that there was a chasm between fact and fiction or, when the reality could not be ignored, justified it as an unfortunate but temporary aberration in the making of a better world.

The use of democratic terminology to justify the repressive and inhumane policies of a totalitarian government served to justify, at least among those who did not know better, the nature and objectives of these policies. At the same time, it further distorted the meaning of democracy, if such were the policies that "democratic" governments could pursue. These Orwellian practices demonstrated the prescience of de Tocqueville's warning that "unless these words ['democracy' and 'democratic government'] are clearly defined and their definition agreed upon, people will live in an inextricable confusion of ideas, much to the advantage of demagogues and despots" (1945:557).

Originally denoting both liberalism and rule by the majority, democracy was subsequently stretched to include nationalism and Stalinist Marxism. The resulting multiplicity of connotations[14] undoubtedly added to democracy's mass appeal. That appeal, however, has carried a very high price. As de Tocqueville feared would happen, the term is now almost devoid of real meaning and consequently susceptible to being used (and grossly misused) in almost any conceivable political sense.[15]

SUMMARY—AND OBITER DICTUM

This chapter has sought to account for the current worldwide popularity of democracy, a popularity that apparently runs counter to our thesis of an innate human bias in favor of authoritarianism. Toward that end, we have made the following points:

1. The present enthusiasm for democracy—or for any other belief—can be viewed as another example of Homo sapiens' unique capacity for self-indoctrination—that is, the ability to create values and then act in pursuit of them, even when those values are inconsistent with or actually opposed to our genetically transmitted behavioral tendencies. Other examples, noted earlier, are the (voluntary) practice of celibacy, the readiness to undergo martyrdom in behalf of one's religious beliefs, and the willingness to die for flag and country.

2. The unremitting hostility of our greatest philosophers to the idea of democratic government, and the actual unpopularity of democratic ideas among the population at large until at least the nineteenth century, are manifestly consistent with what our thesis would predict.[16]

3. The acceptance of democracy was greatly facilitated by the ambiguity of the term. One key component (and the first to win philosophical as well as popular support) argued the existence of natural rights; the other, looking in quite another direction, stressed political equality and majority rule. This combination of essentially incompatible egalitarian and liberal values[17] made it possible for democracy to appeal to quite different groups in the population.

4. Over the last century and a half, both nationalistic political movements and "orthodox" (i.e., Stalinist) Marxism, two of the most potent ideologies of modern times, have employed the symbolism and language of democracy to further their own drastically different agendas. On the one hand, this helped to greatly enlarge democracy's mass following; on the other, it left the term with so many conflicting connotations as to deprive it of almost all substantive meaning. Today, practically any political program, aware of the word's political

cachet, does not hesitate to call itself democratic. In short, the popularity of democracy has waxed as its meaning has waned.[18]

One closely related point remains to be made on the matter of political philosophy. "For the first time in the history of the world," a 1951 UNESCO study enthusiastically reported, "no doctrines are advanced as antidemocratic."

In all probability, quite true.[19] Still, we should not forget that, barely ten years earlier, governments espousing explicitly antidemocratic political beliefs were ruling in Italy, Germany, Spain, Eastern Europe, Latin America, and Asia, to mention only some of the loci. Had there been a UNESCO in the 1930s or even early 1940s, and had it then undertaken a similar study, the ideological balance would have been tipped markedly in the opposite direction. And a UNESCO-type poll two centuries ago would have reported, with probably equal enthusiasm, nearly universal antidemocratic popular sentiments.

Whether we like it or not, not only our philosophers but most of humankind, throughout most of history, have taken it for granted that the few should rule. And, we suggest, despite the lip service presently given to a near vacuous "democracy," they probably continue to do so.

NOTES

1. Note that Dahl here refers to the "idea" rather than the practice of democracy. The practice, he subsequently emphasizes, lags far behind.

2. As Freud somewhere remarked, it is only in logic that contradictions cannot exist.

3. "What we [presently] understand by democracy," Dahl reminds us, "is not what an Athenian in the time of Pericles would have understood by it." The Greek understanding was of direct democracy, and "so deeply held was this view that the Greeks found it difficult to conceive of representative government, much less to accept it as a legitimate alternative to direct democracy" (1989:19). We might also mention the denial of the vote to women, slaves, and non-native-born Athenians.

4. "It is curious that in the abundant literature produced in the greatest democracy in Greece there survives no statement of democratic political theory. All the Athenian political philosophers and publicists whose works we possess were in various degrees oligarchic in sympathy" (Jones, 1940:41). Farrar, we should mention, contends that Protagoras, Thucydides, and Democratus were prodemocratic even though the ideas of these three men "do not look to us like democratic ideas" (1988:2). She later concedes, though, that "There was no . . . direct justification of democracy" (1988:5).

5. "Taking the word democracy in its strict sense, perhaps there never did, and never will, exist such a government. *It is against the natural order that the*

greater number should govern, and the smaller number be governed" (Rousseau, 1973, bk. 3, chap. iv; italics added).

Nor were the spokesmen for the far Left necessarily any more enchanted with democracy. Thus, from Proudhon: "Enough! Let us be frank. Universal suffrage, the popular mandate, the whole elective system is but child's play. I will not trust them with my labor, my peace of mind, my fortune. I will not risk a hair of my head to defend them" (cited by McDonald, 1974:69).

6. "When democracy was first proposed . . . many reasonable people rightly feared it as worse than anarchy" (Kelly, 1994:54).

7. Direct democracy, à la supposed New England town meeting style, is hardly practicable for other than a very small polity.

8. In the twentieth century, the term has experienced almost the same fate as that of "democracy." It is now used in a variety of senses, sometimes to characterize strikingly different ideas and programs. As evidenced in recent American political campaigns, it can apparently be an effective epithet, as if liberalism were a kissing cousin to socialism, if not communism itself. Originally, of course, liberals sought to restrict, rather than expand, the role of government, a position now claimed by the neoliberals.

9. Mill, of course, claimed to rest his defense of human rights on utilitarian rather than natural-law principles.

10. As Norberto Bobbio has cogently observed, "though democracy has . . . been considered as the natural progression from liberalism, the two ideologies prove to be no longer compatible at all once democracy has been taken to its logical extremes as a mass democracy, or rather as a democracy of mass parties" (1987:114). The reason is quite simple: "The ideal of liberal theory was a weak state. The ideal of democratic theory, by contrast, is a powerful state that is controlled by—and thus responsive to—its citizens" (Ginsberg, 1986:5).

11. With the American experience in mind, Dahl (1956) distinguishes between the Madisonian and the populist versions of democracy. The former sought to guard against majority "tyranny" by explicit constitutional prohibitions and the separation of governmental powers. The latter sought to extend the scope of popular sovereignty and regarded any restraints on the will of the majority as a contravention of democratic governance.

12. John Maynard Keynes is alleged to have wondered "how a doctrine so illogical . . . can have exercised so powerful and enduring an influence over the minds of men" (Ulmer, 1987:116).

13. The apparently irresistible temptation to join the notions of nationalism, on the one hand, and democracy, on the other, is nicely illustrated in the boast of French Prime Minister Edouard Balladur that "France . . . has given the rest of the world the concept of the nation and of liberty whose combination underlies our notion of democracy" (*The Economist*, Dec. 2, 1995, p. 62).

14. According to Christopher Lasch, "The word has come to serve simply as a description of the therapeutic state" (1995:6).

15. In all fairness, the American government has not been altogether innocent of this misuse. There comes to mind President Clinton's announced determination, in 1994, to "restore democracy in Haiti." When, we may wonder, did the unfortunate Haitians ever have a government remotely resembling a democracy? Perhaps this type of distortion was what Dwight McDonald had in mind when he spoke of "the meaninglessness of the concept 'democracy' in the modern capitalist world" (1974:366).

16. As is also Arendt's insistence that "mass support for totalitarianism comes neither from ignorance nor from brainwashing" (1966:vii).

17. "Everything in the institutions of democracy," Edward Heimann has warned, "hinges on the reconciliation of liberty and equality" (cited by Dahrendorf, 1968:179).

18. But public opinion favor in these matters is notoriously and demonstrably fickle. Highly regarded but a short time ago, "liberalism" has now become a term of political opprobrium in the United States. Ever adaptable, candidates for public office hasten to assure the electorate that they are not now, nor ever really were, liberals.

Monarchy and aristocracy, have experienced similar reversals from favor to disfavor. If history is a reliable guide, democracy will some day probably suffer the same fate.

19. Well, almost. Using Singapore as the prime but by no means only example, *The Economist* commented on the "general pattern of resistance by Asian leaders to notions about democracy and individual freedoms that most people in the West take as self-evident truths" (Feb. 15, 1992, p. 36). More than three years later, the journal again commented editorially on the "Asian ambivalence about democracy" (July 15, 1995, p. 12).

Part IV

Policy

Chapter 9

Policy Implications

> Whatever the extent or nature of biologically based constraints
> on . . . human behavior, such constraints are most likely to be
> effectively by-passed by humans who . . . are aware of them and
> understand them well.
>   Richard Alexander, "Evolution and Culture," 1979

INTRODUCTION

The proposition that our species has a genetically transmitted tendency to
favor authoritarianism may be doubly disturbing for those who believe (as
we do) that, for all its shortcomings, democracy still remains the best mode
of governance yet devised.[1] Admittedly, such misgivings are justified. On
the one hand, the proposition raises doubts about the continued longevity
of present-day democracies; on the other, it implies that the relative rarity
of democratic polities is likely to be a persistent phenomenon rather than,
as earlier and more optimistic generations thought, merely a stage in
humankind's upward political evolution.[2]

Admittedly, these are conclusions to which our argument would initially
seem to lead.[3] Still, to repeat an earlier caution, a Darwinian approach does
not necessarily result in a counsel of despair. Comprehending the nature of
a problem is an indispensable step toward its possible solution or meliora-
tion. Even Richard Dawkins, whose *The Selfish Gene* is probably the most
sweeping statement of the manner in which genes influence human behavior, shared Richard Alexander's hope (cited at the head of the chapter) that

a better understanding of our biological make-up could be used to counter that influence. "One unique feature of man . . . ," Dawkins reminded his readers,

is his capacity for conscious foresight. . . . We have the power to defy the selfish genes of our birth and, if necessary, the selfish memes of our indoctrination. . . . We are built as gene machines and cultured as meme machines, but we have the power to turn against our creators. We, alone on earth, can rebel. (1989b:200–201)

BEHAVIOR MODIFICATION?

Genetic Engineering, No

How to overcome or, perhaps more realistically, try to obviate this particular evolutionary constraint? Probably the first notion that comes to mind is genetic engineering, à la Aldous Huxley's *Brave New World*. This, however, poses currently insuperable difficulties. Geneticists are still many years distant from a precise knowledge of just how our several million genes interact; and even were the requisite scientific knowledge (and technology) available, there would remain the nearly impossible task of applying it to more than the most trivial fraction of some several billion humans (Barkow, 1989). As a leading British geneticist has recently affirmed, "No serious scientist now has the slightest interest in producing a genetically planned society" (Jones, 1994:225).

But there is a much more powerful objection, especially if our goal is to improve the prospects of successful democracy. Large-scale genetic engineering could be carried out only under governmental auspices. Given the demonstrated readiness of governments and governors to serve their own interests first and best, what citizenry in its right mind—especially in a democracy—would be willing to authorize a policy so blatantly susceptible to political perversion?[4] From a democratic perspective, such a "solution" is worse than the problem itself.

Environmental Engineering, Yes

To rule out genetic engineering does not mean to abandon all hope of modifying our behavior.[5] For centuries, philosophers have debated the relative importance of nature (genes) versus nurture (environment). Contemporary biological thought takes it as axiomatic that this is a false and misleading disjunction: behavior is the product of the interaction between both nature and nurture. Our genes may provide the potential for a given mode of behavior; the environment activates that potential and often significantly influences the manner in which the resulting behavior is displayed and the direction it takes.

In contrast with genetic engineering, we do have the technical capacity to modify our environment and to do so with much less risk. To forestall any possible misunderstanding, let us hastily say that we are speaking here of our intellectual and not our physical environment. With respect to the problem immediately at hand, the prevailing mode of thought with regard to political behavior is characterized by two main tenets: the first holds that political behavior is essentially acquired via a process of socialization; the second sees humanity as innately egalitarian and democratic. Authoritarianism is accordingly viewed as a perversion of, rather than reflection of, our inherent nature.

As Alexander has pointedly observed, "Humans are not accustomed to dealing with their own strategies of life as if they have been tuned by natural selection" (1987:19). And that is precisely the intellectual orientation and perspective that must be changed. We must somehow move toward a much wider popular realization that human behavior is influenced by our genetic legacy and that evolution has endowed us, just as it has the other social primates, with an innate predisposition toward dominance, hierarchy, and obedience. In short, that we are a species inclined toward authoritarian rather than democratic government.

Achieving recognition of this reality is no small task; winning acceptance may be even more difficult.[6] Still, it is not impossible. Some progress has been made in changing popular attitudes toward two other aspects of human behavior—violence and warfare. The prevailing wisdom at midcentury was that humanity was inherently peaceful and that aggression, violence, and war were to be understood as behavioral pathologies spawned by, and arising from, imperfect and malfunctioning political systems. The solution was simple: reform the political system.

That wisdom was directly challenged by the distinguished ethologist Konrad Lorenz, whose *On Aggression* (published in 1966) insisted that humans, as do other animal species, have a "general instinct" for aggressive behavior. Lorenz's contention attracted great popular attention[7] and set off a heated scientific dispute that rages even today.[8] In one sense, the issue has yet to be resolved, for many continue to deny that there is any connection between biology and aggressive behavior or, more commonly, between aggressive behavior, on one level, and warfare, on another. The debate, nonetheless, seems to have resulted in a definite change in the popular and scientific understanding of aggressive behavior, now increasingly viewed as an inherent tendency of human—and especially male—behavior.[9] To that degree, the intellectual environment in which discussions of aggression, violence, and warfare have taken place and possible "solutions" advanced has been progressively modified.

The current campaigns against racial and sexual discrimination may offer even closer analogs, since both entail deliberate attempts to change long-established behaviors. In both, the fundamental objective has been to sensitize the public and public officials not only to the pervasiveness but the costly consequences, to society as well as the individual, of these behaviors. Such an awareness, the campaigners know, is the key to the eventual success of their efforts.

There are, to be sure, some points of difference. Scientific opinion is still divided on whether sexual and/or racial discrimination can be satisfactorily explained by socialization (i.e., human indoctrinability) alone or whether it may reflect some underlying genetic tendency.[10] Beyond this, it is possible to pass laws and to establish policies that prohibit and punish those forms of discrimination. The existence and enforcement of these laws can, of itself, serve to affect some of these behaviors, though not necessarily the attitudes from which they spring. To accomplish that kind of attitudinal change will require a long process of education and enlightenment.

A similar, and perhaps even more far-reaching, modification of our intellectual environment will have to be accomplished with regard to Homo sapiens' genetic pro-authoritarian bias. There is little likelihood of winning public support for political strategies and policies designed to counter and offset that bias (or for those strategies and policies to have any chance of success) until their evolutionary origins are much more widely understood and accepted. That will require the kind of ongoing debate and discussion that Lorenz set into motion with regard to aggression, which we are now witnessing in the areas of sexual and racial discrimination.[11]

But we should not underestimate the magnitude and difficulty of the task. Survey after survey shows that the majority of the American population still either does not believe in or has serious doubts about evolution. Many of those who accept it in principle still deny its applicability to humans. The subject is totally ignored in many school systems; in others, it is present as simply one of several competing theories rather than as a scientifically accepted phenomenon. Thus, the Alabama State Board of Education recently (November 1995) ordained that any textbook discussing the topic must include an insert describing evolution as "a controversial theory some scientists present as a scientific explanation for the origin of living things" (Holden, 1995:1305). The battle to teach evolution in American public grade and high schools continues, with uncertain prospects in the face of a rising tide of Christian, Jewish, and Islamic fundamentalism.

Although the teaching of evolution at the college level is much less susceptible to political pressure, there are other limiting factors. Even today, only half of our youth go on to some form of higher education; of these, only half will complete the baccalaureate. At many colleges, for whatever reason, evolution is still not part of the required curriculum. And although knowledge of evolutionary theory is more widespread among college graduates than among the population at large, a sizable proportion of the graduates are either ignorant of or reject neo-Darwinian ideas.

Admittedly, the battle remains to be won. Nevertheless, the intellectual environment can be changed. Motion pictures, television and radio programming, the print media—all surely aimed at a mass audience—testify that evolutionary ideas are gradually achieving greater popular acceptance. Conceivably, the balance may ultimately tip. If and when that happens, we will have taken a major step toward altering our intellectual environment and, with a bit of luck, perhaps eventually even our political behavior. We can only hope that this book, and others seeking to refute or support it, will play some part in moving that process along.

Now to more specific policy proposals, aimed at more immediate objectives and, we like to think, capable of more immediate implementation. Understandably, we will cast these in terms of the American situation, although the same suggestions might warrant consideration in other democracies as well. The problems we will be reviewing are not limited to the North American continent, as Lipset has recently observed, "Ironically, the victory of the democracies in the Cold War has been followed by a decline in their major democratic institutions" (1995:6).

What, then, might such policies entail? In the following discussion we will deal first with foreign and then with domestic policy. In real life, to be sure, the two are often closely interrelated, since governmental actions in the international arena are so frequently influenced by domestic political considerations. Nonetheless, we are on reasonably safe ground in distinguishing between them conceptually and, for our purposes, operationally.

We start with foreign policy for essentially tactical reasons. Although our proposals under this heading are not likely to be particularly palatable for many of our readers, they will be much less objectionable, we suspect, than those advanced in our discussion of domestic policy.

FOREIGN POLICY

Democratic and Republican administrations alike have repeatedly declared that one of their major objectives has been to encourage and assist democratic governments around the world. Ideological empathies aside, the basic justification has been that such a course is in our "national interest," that is, that it is to the United States' advantage to do so.[12]

It is by no means evident, though, that our national interest has actually been appreciably advanced by this professed policy. First of all, the chances of success are quite small. Democracies, a rare species historically, are still uncommon today. In part this is because of our species' inherent authoritarian bias, in part because of the absence of many, if not most, of the material conditions regarded as indispensable requisites for the establishment of a viable democratic political system.

Given these two major obstacles, the results of our democracy-building ventures have not been very heartening. The vast outpourings of American financial and other assistance notwithstanding (see later discussion), only a small handful of nations have made the transition from authoritarianism to democracy since 1945; in most cases, there is as yet distressingly little to show for our efforts.[13]

Furthermore, almost everyone who has studied the subject agrees that the birth and successful survival of a democracy[14] is far more likely to depend upon endogenous[15] rather than exogenous factors[16] (Barro and Saint Martin, 1995). Since 1945 there have been very few instances where American intervention and/or assistance can plausibly be claimed to have played a significant, let alone a decisive, role in the emergence of a viable democracy.

Japan—despite its almost unbroken post–World War II tradition of one-party government—is perhaps the best example of such a success; Germany[17] is somewhat less so, since there already existed there the rudiments of a quasi-democratic political past on which to build. Finally, there is Israel, which, although a democracy from the start, almost surely would not have survived its fanatically hostile neighbors in the absence of massive American military and financial help. These countries aside, where else has American assistance helped a democratic government emerge?[18]

Third, un-American as the idea may appear, attempting to help nascent democracies elsewhere may not always be in our own best interests.[19] To begin, for the reasons noted above, the effort is unlikely to be fruitful. Furthermore, the resources expended in these various undertakings might have yielded a greater return, in terms of strengthening democracy, if invested at home. Although "only" about $15 billion is presently being allocated annually for foreign aid, this was not always the case. Since 1947, we have spent somewhere between $1.2 and $1.5 *trillion* on "international development and humanitarian assistance" and "international security assistance" (*Congressional Quarterly*, December 17, 1994; p. 3568).[20] Arguably, this vast outpouring of money could be justified as compelled by cold war objectives, or humanitarian considerations, or on the grounds of economic self-interest. That, though, is quite a different matter from the claim that outlays to encourage democratic development in other nations are necessarily in our national interest.

One other point should be made at this juncture. Even in those few instances where our efforts may have played a decisive role, the outcomes did not work to further our national interest in all respects. Consider, for instance, Japan and Germany, which, quite reasonably from their perspective, soon began to pursue social, economic, and political policies often at variance with our own—and in some instances strikingly more successful than ours. Nor, to take another familiar example, is there necessarily any identity between what the United States and Israel, respectively, would consider to be a satisfactory resolution of present-day Middle Eastern issues (Ben-Zvi, 1994).

These and other differences were surely predictable. "National interests" (or the current operational definition thereof) inevitably vary from one nation to another, whatever their ideological and governmental similarities. Unquestionably, these three countries were profoundly grateful for the help we provided. Still, as many historians have remarked—and many politicians belatedly discovered—gratitude among nations has a remarkably short half-life.[21]

We are not saying that U.S. foreign policy should never seek to assist existing or, more likely, emerging democracies around the world. We are saying, however, that supporting democracy elsewhere may not necessarily be the best way to advance our national interest. This means that when such support is provided:

1. It should be done very selectively, after a realistically dispassionate cost-benefit analysis, not on the basis of a characteristically optimistic "let's try" rationalization. The parallel that inevitably comes to mind here is the $5.3 trillion devoted to antipoverty programs since 1965—and the continuing persistence, possibly even worsening, of poverty as a major national problem.

2. If and when we decide to make such an attempt, it should be with an explicit awareness that, for the reasons described above, it will probably be unsuccessful. For example, attempts to overthrow an existing despotic regime are more likely to eventuate in the establishment of a successor government just as authoritarian as its predecessor than in a democratic polity.

3. In any given country, internal conditions and forces are more important in determining the outcome than is outside assistance (barring actual military intervention). And military interventions, we have repeatedly seen, can have most unpredictable outcomes.

4. In many instances, our national interest might be better advanced by some alternative—though perhaps politically less sexy—domestic utilization of the funds. Quite a few school lunches, to mention only one spendthrift option, could be purchased for a fraction of the $15 billion currently (1995) allocated for foreign aid.

5. In the case, however unlikely, that a new democracy actually does emerge as a consequence of our efforts, it will soon develop goals and objectives that differ from, or even clash with, those we espouse.

6. The use of boycotts, embargoes, the threat to withdraw "most favored nation" status, and so forth, all presumably in the interest of encouraging greater democratization and concern for human rights, has in almost every instance failed to achieve any of its desired effects. Except, that is, to benefit other, competing nations who observe with some bemusement (and commercial gain) our remarkable readiness to shoot ourselves, economically speaking, in at least one foot.

All of this suggests that we would serve American democracy best by limiting our efforts to foster democracy elsewhere to those few instances where there is some reasonable prospect of success—that is, to nations where some of the requisite material conditions already exist. Relatively few of the countries that have been the beneficiaries of American largesse come close to satisfying these conditions.

The recommendation that the United States should think not twice but several times before trying to export democracy to other countries is manifestly less controversial and consequently more likely of possible implementation than would have been the case a bare decade ago. As already remarked, American expenditures under the general headings of international development and humanitarian assistance as well as international security assistance have fallen very sharply in recent years.

There were several reasons for that decline. Among the most important, if not the foremost, was the political reality that in an era of increasing budgetary stringency, slashing foreign aid was far less likely to evoke electoral retribution than cutting sizable chunks from some domestic program or programs. The willingness to cut back on democratization efforts was further strengthened by a growing scholarly literature that, as we earlier noted, called attention to the failures of that policy to achieve its purported objectives and/or argued that the success or failure of democracy in a given nation was primarily a function of internal rather than external factors.

At the same time, there was a growing if belated public recognition that democracies could not speedily be built on the ruins of toppled totalitarian regimes. Repeated setbacks in Central and Eastern Europe made it evident that the task of constructing a viable democracy was immeasurably more complex and difficult than imagined during the mass and media euphoria which followed the collapse of the Soviet Union. As that tardy realization crystallized, the idea of investing American resources to assist in so precarious and uncertain an undertaking—especially during a period when budget cutting had become a, if not *the*, major national priority—understandably had little popular support.

Finally, there was a series of unhappy foreign policy experiences, ranging from the failure to achieve a satisfactory closure from the war with Iraq to the fiascoes and disasters experienced by the United States and its allies in Bosnia, Somalia, Rwanda, and so forth. These tragic developments encouraged a resurgence of the isolationist sentiment that has so long been an aspect of American political life—and that played no small role in both the 1994 congressional election and in the legislation subsequently proposed by the victorious Republican leadership in both the House and the Senate.

All of these factors, reinforcing each other, have been operative in bringing about a significant reduction in American expenditures of money, material and manpower designed to help build democracies elsewhere. Ironically, though, while the change in policy has been in the direction we have suggested, some of the reasons underlying that shift—isolationism is the most obvious example—have ample potential for future mischief.

The touchstone to be applied when faced with the temptation to try to help democracy elsewhere, we would argue, is whether the proposed assistance or intervention has a realistic chance of achieving its objective. In the great majority of instances, prior experience suggests, the answer will be clearly no. If, however, realistic analysis suggests otherwise, then we should consider another frequently ignored question: given the substantial costs—economic, political, diplomatic, and so forth—inevitably inherent in any such venture, is the projected action really in our national interest? As a recent *Economist* article would have it, "The 'expansion of democracy' is of course a desirable if imprecise objective for American foreign policy, but it is not a critical one. Democracy comes in uneven measures, and it is not the prime consideration in Ukraine, for example, or Saudi Arabia" (May 26, 1995, p. 23). There are ineluctable limits not only to what we can, but to what we should attempt to accomplish.

IMPLICATIONS FOR DOMESTIC POLICY

> American democracy is in much deeper trouble than most people wish to acknowledge. . . . What exists behind the formal shell is a systemic breakdown of the shared civic values we call democracy.
> William Greider, *Who Will Tell the People?*, 1992

We will focus here, naturally, on strengthening the American democracy. The importance of this objective, though, reaches far beyond our borders: the decline or failure of democracy in the United States would gravely undermine prospects for its continued viability elsewhere in the contemporary world. Furthermore, some of the problems we will be discussing are not uniquely American—and the policies suggested may well have relevance for other democracies.

From a neo-Darwinian perspective, what measures are essential to ensure the survival of democracy in this country? We argued earlier that, despite our species' innate hierarchical bias, democracy is occasionally made possible by a fortuitous conjunction of that unique human attribute, indoctrinability, and the necessary but of themselves not sufficient enabling social, economic, and other, conditions. To be successful, then, efforts to strengthen American democracy must take adequate cognizance of all three of these factors—our authoritarian genetic legacy, our capacity for indoctrination, and the importance of the aforementioned socioeconomic conditions.

The Basic Requisites for Democracy: Going, Going . . .

Democratic institutions, the experts concur, are not likely to survive, let alone flourish, absent certain facilitating social and economic conditions (Diamond, Linz, and Lipset, 1990; Putnam, 1993, 1995a, 1995b). It is with these, then, that we should start: What is the necessary combination of these requisite enabling or facilitating factors? What is the relative importance of each?

Social scientists are still unable to specify the exact mix (or mixes) that somehow interact to constitute the proper critical mass. Nonetheless, there is nearly unanimous agreement that in the absence of any significant number of these factors, democracy is likely neither to emerge nor, where already existent, to long survive.

The problem that immediately concerns us is that many of these essential conditions are being steadily eroded in the United States. We refer, holding the litany to a bare minimum, to the following:

- The growing number of Americans (and of children in particular)[22] who live in poverty

- The emergence of what many fear is a quasi-permanent, largely unemployable underclass

- The vast and widening differences in wealth and in life experiences between our upper and lower socioeconomic classes[23]

- The failures of our educational system[24] and the functional illiteracy of so many high school and even college graduates[25]

- Worsening racial tensions, now expanded to include relations involving Hispanics and Asians as well as relations between whites and blacks

- The decline in political participation as measured by the simple act of voting

- The lack of information and interest in civic matters among our teenagers[26]

- The growing strength of religious and political fundamentalism characterized by an angry intolerance of dissenting opinions[27]

- Political campaigns that rely heavily on mudslinging[28] and "30-second sound byte" television and media trivializations (Fallows, 1996)

- The staggering cost of seeking public office[29] and the resulting influence of those who can contribute generously to campaign funds

- A political pluralism dominated by self-centered interest groups

- The dangerous erosion of what Putnam (1995a) calls the "social capital" that has made American democracy possible

- A political system that is seemingly incapable of coming to grips with urgent political issues—even after the so-called revolution of 1994.

Individually, these are all serious matters. But the problem runs much deeper: Collectively, these developments are undermining and threatening to destroy the conditions that have historically made democracy possible. We are perilously close to losing the key constituent elements, to borrow Vaclav Havel's (1987, 1990) now classic phrase, of a democratic "civil society."[30]

If this is the case, we seem to be faced with three possible outcomes. Scenario 1 is that democracy can and will somehow survive in the absence of most, if not all, of what have hitherto been its essential enabling conditions. Theoretically conceivable, yes; from a historical perspective, looking at the fate of democracies from the Roman Republic to the present,[31] such a happy resolution would appear to be rather improbable.[32]

In Scenario 2, the conditions traditionally associated with democracy are eventually eroded—and the United States, either gradually or in some sudden convulsion à la Sinclair Lewis's *It Can't Happen Here*, undergoes a transformation to a more authoritarian mode of government. As between the first and second scenarios, this latter is perhaps the more likely, though certainly the less attractive, of the two.

Scenario 3 has the American democracy belatedly demonstrating the ability to stop and in some instances even reverse many of these threatening social, economic, and political trends. Certainly there has been no paucity either of proposals or of disagreements about the measures that government might take.[33] These disagreements are troublesome enough in themselves. But the resulting (from a popular perception) systemic paralysis has given rise to an even more serious problem—a growing belief that our democratic mode of governance is now simply incapable of dealing with issues of this magnitude.

In the face of this spreading disaffection, one is almost tempted to say that it may now be less important that government make exactly the right decision than that it demonstrate a willingness and a capacity to act on urgent issues. Kevin Phillips succinctly summarized the danger when he warned that "from the White House to Capitol Hill, a critical weakness in American politics and governance is becoming woefully apparent—the frightening inability of the nation's leaders to face, much less define and debate, the unprecedented problems and opportunities facing the country" (1990:ix).

Needless to say, Scenario 3 would be the happiest outcome. For this to occur, though, the American political system would have to do more than tackle the problems that we have identified. It would also have to formulate and put into effect a successful policy for taking advantage of the second of the two factors that make democracy viable. We refer, in case the reader has forgotten, to Homo sapiens' unique capacity for indoctrinability.

This is not a capacity that our nation can any longer afford to leave, as Milton urged, to the "free and open encounter"[34] of the ideological market-place. And that brings us to what will almost assuredly be, from a traditional liberal outlook, the most distasteful of our neo-Darwinian recommendations.

Civic Indoctrination: The Need for a National Policy

Given its evolutionary origins, ours is a hierarchically rather than a democratically inclined species. We have evolved, though, at least one other capacity that sets us apart from all the other social primates—indoctrinability. Indoctrinability endows ideas and values with the power to alter profoundly the behaviors of those who believe in them. As earlier emphasized, once accepted, these ideas and values can triumph even over those behaviors—and sex, violence, and dominance are the most obvious examples—to which Homo sapiens are otherwise naturally predisposed.

The occasional emergence of democratic government, we have argued, can be attributed to a fortuitous combination of indoctrinability and favorable social, economic, and political conditions. To survive, a democracy must continue to meet both of these requirements. That is, the requisite social, economic, and other conditions must be maintained—and democratic indoctrination must somehow be effectively accomplished. Over the past two decades or so, the American democracy has increasingly failed to ensure the first, and from the beginning of the post–World War II era, it has been abysmally deficient in satisfying the second of these requirements. This latter problem now also imperatively demands corrective action.

The Case for a National Policy of Democratic Indoctrination

Almost all governments utilize their public (and to the degree possible their private) schools to inculcate in their young a belief in the virtues of the existent political order. Although other instruments of indoctrination are also regularly employed, the initial and primary responsibility for this task is almost always assigned to the educational system.

Totalitarian polities, as we have so often seen, invest very heavily in this objective, seeking unquestioned ideological acceptance and conveying to the young an unfavorable understanding of rival ideologies and the countries by which they are espoused. Democracies, too, seek to indoctrinate their youth. In sharp contrast, though, democratic states are characterized by— and take pride in—the relatively free play they permit within their schools in the discussion of diverse and even antithetical political ideas and regimes.

American practice in this matter can be sketched in broad strokes. From the Pilgrim fathers onward, church-affiliated schools at all levels paid great attention to religious and moral training. This concern, in fact, provided much of the impetus for the establishment of schools and is often still reflected in their curricula today.

Understandably, systematic civic indoctrination, that is, teaching the young the merits of republican democracy, did not begin until much later; the Jacksonian era might be a convenient dating point. From then until World War I, the public schools fulfilled this responsibility quite effectively, especially when we take into consideration the multitude (some 30 million plus) and diversity of immigrants who poured into the country after the Civil War. By almost any criterion, the schools (evening and day) were remarkably successful in Americanizing the newly arrived immigrants and their many more millions of children, as well as in transmitting to both an understanding of and appreciation for the American political way of life.

Very few questioned the merits of that undertaking. By and large, as Elshtain observes, "it was taken for granted from the start of the American democratic experiment that the survival of the republic for any length of time would depend heavily on the cultivation of civic sentiments among the young" (1995:78) and that the inculcation of these sentiments was a major and proper function of public education. Thus, to offer only one of innumerable examples, an 1885 University of Iowa commencement speaker could impassionately declare that "our University owes its existence to the government. Let her pay the debt by teaching its principles, its history, its purposes, its duties, its privileges, and its powers" (Crick, 1960:23).

Early in the twentieth century, though, attitudes about the desirability of using the schools as instruments of civic indoctrination began to change.[35] Inevitably, as attitudes changed, the schools' concern with and effectiveness in teaching the virtues of the American democracy began to diminish, slowly at first and then, after World War II, with increasing rapidity. By the early 1950s, a deepening sense that the American educational system was failing in this respect elicited the concern of two major educational groups. In 1952, the National Educational Association, describing the schools as "a bulwark against the dangers of disloyalty," urged a much more effective teaching of "American values" for both men and women. Two years later, the American Association of School Administrators called upon the schools to "teach and defend the ideals of American society and to produce strong-minded Americans devoted to democracy" (Hepburn, 1990:156).

Whatever gains these recommendations might have produced were soon negated by the furious reaction against the Vietnam War, possibly the most massive expression of political protest in American history. The resulting disaffection barely had time to subside when the sordid Watergate revelations began. These two epochal events profoundly affected how a large number of Americans viewed their government; beyond question, they profoundly colored the thinking of many of the youth who eventually went on to constitute a majority of our present-day grade school, high school, and college teachers.[36]

More recently, the idea that democratic civic indoctrination is a proper educational function has been implicitly and sometimes explicitly rejected by multiculturalism, a concept that became increasingly popular among educators over the past few decades. In principle, multiculturalism seeks to teach students about other cultures, other peoples, other religions, other political doctrines, other ways of looking at the world. In practice, though, multiculturalism often has entailed uncritical praise of other cultures[37] and a disparaging discussion of what are termed "Eurocentric," "white," "racist," "sexist," "capitalist," and "homophobic" ideas, art, and institutions.[38] And often subsumed under this heading is democracy, American style.

No wonder that our schools—beset by multiculturalism on one flank, by Deweyites and by Miltonian believers in "free and open encounters" on another, by proponents of "life adjustment education" on yet a third,[39] and confronted with almost daily media exposures of governmental deceit, ineptitude, and corruption—have in so many instances either abandoned or simply been unable to carry out their earlier responsibility for civic education. Nor is it surprising, given recent American history and the current intellectual climate, that one result has been "the cynicism and even contempt with which so many people view our political institutions and leaders" (McNamara, 1995).

Governments in small states, such as Haiti, before "democracy," and sometimes those in larger Third World countries can maintain themselves in power by relying almost totally upon force and fear. The great majority of political regimes, though, depend upon some combination of popular acceptance (or tolerance) and coercion to perpetuate themselves in office.[40] In principle if not always in practice, the greater the degree of perceived legitimacy, the less the need for threat and force. Consequently, even authoritarian and totalitarian regimes strive mightily to keep alive in their subjects that sense of legitimacy. Still, even the most strenuous of these efforts have their limits. As most recently evidenced in Eastern Europe, once the gap between the official version of reality and what the citizens actually experience and can tolerate exceeds a certain point, that government is doomed and its demise is simply a matter of time.

Democracies, by their very nature, rely far less on force and fear and much more heavily on ideological acceptance. Because of this, they must solve a number of problems not usually encountered by other forms of government. First, as already emphasized, we are by our genetic endowment inclined to favor authoritarian ideas. Inculcating the citizenry with the virtues of political equality is thus both more important and more difficult than is the task of civic indoctrination in other, more hierarchically organized political societies.

Second, democracies require special conditions for their birth and survival; authoritarian regimes, in contrast, can take root and flourish in practically any environment. A significant decline in, or deterioration of, these enabling conditions thus poses a much more serious threat to a democratic government than to an authoritarian one.

Third, the freedom of discussion and political action that characterizes democracies enables those who preach other ideologies to make maximum capital of any shortcomings, actual or merely alleged, of the democratic system. The very openness of democratic polities almost guarantees that real or seeming disparities between the promises of democratic ideology and the reality of democratic performance will speedily be called to public attention.

For all of these reasons, effective civic indoctrination is even more essential in a democracy than in other types of political societies. It is important even when things are going well; it is absolutely critical when the democracy is experiencing serious difficulties.

That, unhappily, is exactly where we are in the United States today. The social and economic conditions that make democracy possible have become dangerously attenuated; these problems simply must be addressed and corrected.

No less threatening, sizable segments of our citizenry are disenchanted with, or clearly alienated from, our democratic political system. This development, too, must be addressed and corrected. In short, this means that civic indoctrination, especially of the young, is not something that can any longer be left to chance. It is, rather, a matter that urgently demands national action and a national policy. The federal government, in concert with the states, must devise a policy aimed to inculcate in our youth an intelligent appreciation of democratic governance—and then provide, as needed, the resources required for the policy to be successfully implemented.

The objectives of such a policy, we think, should be twofold:

1. To ensure that students are given a basic understanding of American history and the manner in which our governmental system functions. These subjects are already part of the curricula of most of our schools, but numerous studies indicate that students too often complete their education incredibly ill-informed in both of these areas. The goals here would be to improve, where necessary, the content and the quality of what are generally termed "civics" courses and to inculcate in the students a favorable but by no means uncritical perception of democracy in general and the American democracy in particular.[41]

2. To convey an understanding of the history of democracy and of democratic theory, of the difference not merely of political form but of substantive political life between authoritarian and democratic governments, of the special problems faced by democracies, and, consequently, of their unique fragility. This material should not be taught in terms of abstract political concepts but should be directly related to current issues faced by the United States and, where relevant, to other contemporary democratic polities.

This is precisely the type of understanding of other cultures and other peoples purportedly sought by proponents of multiculturalism. The great difference is that the proposed policy would seek to ensure that students attain the same understanding of the merits and special virtues, as well as the faults and shortcomings, of their own government. The evidence strongly suggests that this second objective is being neither pursued nor achieved in most of our public schools.

There are at least two aspects of this proposal, we realize, that many will find highly objectionable. One is that we deliberately use our schools as instruments for democratic indoctrination; the other is that education, hitherto a province reserved to the states, should become a matter of federal policy and action.

Despite abundant evidence that our schools have historically served a political purpose, the issue of whether the schools *should* be instruments of social indoctrination has long been debated by American educators. Some 60 years ago, in challenging the opposition of Deweyites to "teaching democracy," George Counts reminded them that

all education contains a large amount of imposition [of social values], that in the very nature of the case this is inevitable, that the existence and evolution of society depend on it, that it is consequently eminently desirable, and that the frank acceptance of this fact by the educator is a major professional obligation. (cited in Raywid, 1980:4)

Even John Dewey, who initially opposed the idea, eventually conceded that indoctrination was a proper function of the schools if the result "is at least a self-correcting indoctrination, not one which demands the subordination of critical discrimination and comparison" (cited in Raywid, 1980:8–9).

There is no point in retracing this controversy, one that has generated a huge, often highly polemical, literature that continues to expand at the rate of some half-dozen items annually. Whether we like it or not, societies—as Counts insisted—simply must indoctrinate their young. We must choose, therefore, between doing it poorly, as is currently the case, or doing it well. Admittedly, there are dangers entailed. Nonetheless, the history of American education until well into the twentieth century demonstrates that it is possible to conduct effective civic indoctrination and, at the same time, to teach students how to think critically about social and political matters.

Rather curiously, those who are most vehemently opposed to civic indoctrination are often those who want the schools to conduct sex education or to teach the folly of drinking, smoking, and using drugs. But attitudes on this issue may be undergoing a profound change. Just as these paragraphs were being written, one of our most influential educational institutions, the Carnegie Corporation, advanced a series of recommendations that, taking for granted that civic indoctrination is one of their major responsibilities, urge American schools to assume a much more active role in transmitting social and moral values.

A second and quite different objection to the proposed national policy is that under the American Constitution, education is not a power granted to the federal government; historically, this function has been reserved to the states, and in fact, traditionally it has been carried out by them,[42] not by the federal government. This may once have been the case. In recent decades, however, the federal government, via grants-in-aid, civil rights legislation, and court decisions, has profoundly influenced education at all levels. In any event, our proposal would leave operational responsibility for civic education with the states. Their cooperation would be sought, first, by their participation in the formulation of the policy, and second, via a by now familiar combination of fiscal carrots and sticks.

One other major objection, not philosophical, not legal, but strictly practical, remains to be considered. This is the contention that whatever the merits of the proposed policy, it cannot be successfully implemented. The reason advanced is quite simple—our school systems, especially those in urban areas where the task of indoctrination is probably the most difficult, are no more capable of meeting this challenge than they are of providing their students with more than the barest rudiments of an education. Even worse, the argument continues, our schools have shown that they are essentially incapable of reforming themselves in other than cosmetic fashion.

Unfortunately, this is not an objection that can be dismissed out of hand. We need hardly dwell here on the shortcomings of our big (and often small) city public schools—and the near illiteracy of so many of their graduates. It is also true that, in almost all instances, attempts to reform these schools have produced little in the way of tangible results.[43]

Any national policy aimed at effective civic indoctrination will certainly have to take this distressingly stubborn reality into account. In fact, one consequence of such a policy could be a more successful restructuring of the American educational system than anything attempted to date. What we have not been able to bring about at the local (and even state) level, using admittedly limited resources, might be accomplished if pursued on a national scale with the support of the federal government.

Can we design and carry out a national policy of effective civic education? In all candor, we do not know. But that is really not the key question. What we must ask is this: If the American democracy is to be preserved, do we have any choice other than to make the attempt?

NOTES

1. Or, as Winston Churchill put it, "Democracy is the worst form of government—except for all the others."

2. Thus, according to Victor Hugo, "Every civilization begins in theocracy and ends in democracy."

3. It was precisely this reaction that Irenaus Eibl-Eibesfeldt, probably Europe's preeminent ethologist, had in mind when he wrote "But what is the main reason for rejecting the idea of biological factors in human behavior? . . . [I]t is the fear that biologically determined factors are unalterable, impregnable, and uncontrollable" (1979:165).

4. Innumerable science fiction authors, especially since *Brave New World*, have explored the possible, and almost invariably unattractive, outcomes of such a policy.

5. "The value of an evolutionary approach . . . is thus not to determine the limits of our actions so that we can abide by them. Rather, it is to examine our life strategies so that we can change them when we wish, as a result of our understanding them" (Alexander, 1987:9–10).

6. "The search for the [evolutionary] bases of human sociality, unlike those for the physical base of the universe . . . is a quest that, again unlike that of the theoretical physicists, leads not merely to skepticism but to hostility, fear, resistance and even bitter and vituperative rejections" (Alexander, 1987:31).

7. For this, Robert Ardrey's *Territorial Imperative* and *Social Contract* deserve considerable credit.

8. The resulting controversy has produced a truly formidable ethological and sociobiological literature. See, for instance, Eibl-Eibesfeldt (1979), Shaw and Wong (1989), Van der Dennen and Falger (1990). The 1990 "Seville Statement," which sought flatly to contradict Lorenz, has created an entire subliterature of its own (see, for instance, Scott and Ginsberg [1994]).

9. Lorenz, we might say, lost the battle but won the war. His "hydraulic" model explanation has since been essentially rejected—and his base contention, largely accepted.

10. The answers may ultimately differ. At the moment, a somewhat stronger case can be made for a genetic bias in racial than in sexual discrimination.

11. And, almost needless to say, in the efforts to end discrimination against gays and lesbians.

12. It is sometimes difficult to escape the suspicion that incumbent administrations, Democratic and Republican alike, sometimes define the national interest in terms of their own perceived political advantage.

13. How much progress, it may be fair to ask, toward democratic governance in the Middle East, presumably one of our objectives, was made by the outcome of the Gulf War?

14. Except, of course, when threatened by external forces, as in the case of the invasion of Hungary.

15. Analyzing the experiences of thirty-five countries that have attempted to move from authoritarianism to democracy since 1974, Huntington (1991) has derived a set of guidelines designed to assist future "democratizers."

16. To be sure, Allison and Beschel (1992) argue that "the evidence suggests that in fact the United States has promoted democracy and is promoting democracy" (1992:82). In support of their contention, they list "fifty-seven specific . . . actions the U.S. government can take or refrain from in order to promote democracy." (1992:82) Unfortunately, with two exceptions, the two authors neglect to show (1) that the United States has in the past undertaken such actions, and, perhaps still more to the point, (2) that even if undertaken, they had any notable impact on the course of events. The two instances they offer to support their position, interestingly enough, are Nicaragua and the Philippines. Ah, with democracies like these, who needs autocracies?

17. More precisely, originally West Germany.

18. In fact, a plausible case can be made that American foreign policy in Latin America during the decades of the cold war, whatever our professed intentions, did at least as much to deter as to foster the development of democratic governance. For example, whatever one thinks of the Arbenz (Guatemala) and Allende (Chile) regimes, they were democratically elected and the United States played an active part in destabilizing and destroying them. In both instances, dictatorships followed.

Currently, the United States is expending great effort to create and—if the creation works—to maintain democracy in Haiti. The outcome of this experiment, we fear, will only further support our thesis.

19. Though based on quite a different line of reasoning, this is much the same conclusion voiced by Ronald Steel (1995) in arguing for what one reviewer called a "minimalist foreign policy."

20. Senator Jesse Helms, a not unbiased critic, puts the total at $2 trillion (*Congressional Quarterly*, December 17, 1994, p. 3569). Neither of these figures includes the cost of the Korean and Vietnam wars.

21. Of course, anyone who has taken seriously Hans Morgenthau's "realist" view of foreign policy would hardly be surprised.

22. Recent estimates are that one child in three comes from a family living below the poverty line. On March 29, 1995, the Associated Press carried a story opening with the sentence, "Children born to poor, black women and to uneducated mothers of all races are more likely than others to be mildly retarded, federal researchers reported yesterday." For recent—and divergent—contributions to the discussion of poverty in America, see Madrick (1995) and Samuelson (1996).

23. "George Bush's wonderment, when he saw for the first time, an electronic scanning device at a supermarket check-out counter, revealed, as in a flash of lightning, the chasm that divides the privileged classes from the rest of the nation" (Lasch, 1995:4).

24. For the most recent additions to an already overlarge literature, see Sykes (1996), Berliner and Biddle (1996), and Tyack and Cuban (1996).

25. See, for example, *A Nation at Risk*, National Commission on Excellence in Education, 1983. Herrnstein and Murray (1994:417) advance a somewhat different view, arguing that "a search of the data does not reveal that the typical American

school child in the past would have done any better on tests of academic skills." The real change, rather, has been what they term the "dumbing down" of the education received by the top 20 percent of American students. Summarizing a recent Organization for Economic Cooperation and Development (OECD) study of reading comprehension, the ability to read maps, and the ability to deal with everyday math problems, *The Economist* reported that "in all, Americans did better than Poland but worse than anyone else" (December 9, 1995, p. 27).

26. "The proportion of college freshmen who say that paying close attention to political affairs is important has declined to its lowest level in the 20 years that freshman attitudes have been surveyed" (*International Herald Tribune,* January 10, 1995, p. 3).

27. "We citizens of the United States are told by the young and the angry and the old . . . that it is no longer possible for us to speak to one another; that we, quite literally, inhabit our own islands of bristling indifference where we comport with those just like ourselves; no outsiders are welcome" (Elshtain, 1995:xi). Or, as Lasch sees it, "In practice, diversity turns out to legitimate a new dogmatism, in which rival minorities take shelter behind a set of beliefs impervious to rational discussion" (1995:17).

28. In addition to its short-run effect, this type of campaigning appears to undermine attitudes important for a democracy (Ansolabehere et al., 1994:829–838).

29. As of 1995, a congressional election campaign generally required a minimum of $3 to $5 million, although one of the California candidates for a Senate seat was reported to have spent some $20 million—and his successful rival a bit less. Pundits estimate that it will take at least $30 to $40 million to mount a (possibly) successful campaign for the 2000 Republican presidential nomination. Once the candidate is nominated, there would, of course, be the cost of the presidential campaign itself.

30. For a more detailed discussion, see Elshtain (1995:5–21).

31. We start with Rome because a plausible, if not persuasive, case can be made that Athenian democracy died from exogenous causes (the defeat by Sparta, etc.) rather than endogenous ones.

32. One might argue, of course, that given the small number of democracies the world has known, the set of those that have fallen is too small to permit any really firm conclusion.

33. In the past half-dozen years alone, to mention only a fraction of these efforts, there have been Cheney (1990), Dionne (1991), Elshtain (1995), Etzioni (1993), Jacoby (1994), Kaus (1992), Lasch (1995), Oldenburg (1989), Reich (1992), and Steinem (1992). Discussing the pros and cons of these proposals and seeking to identify those that seem most promising would require another book, undoubtedly much larger than this one. The task of devising a political strategy whereby such a program might have some realistic chance of enactment would probably entail an additional, no less sizable, volume.

34. "And though all the winds of doctrine were let loose to play on the earth, so truth be in the field, we do injuriously by licensing and prohibiting to misdoubt her strength. Let her and falsehood grapple; who ever knew truth to be put to the worse in a free and open encounter?" (Milton, 1992:27)

However commendable his philosophical values, Milton was wrong in his reading of history. Five thousand years of recorded history attest that the battle between democratic and nondemocratic political ideas is rarely, if ever, a "free and open encounter." To begin, the ideological playing field is tilted by our genetic inclinations toward authoritarianism; with few exceptions, the terrain is made still more uneven by the superior resources of those who, in most polities, have ample cause to oppose democratic ideas and democratic governance alike.

35. Many factors undoubtedly contributed to this attitudinal shift. Among the most obvious of these are: (1) the influence of John Dewey and his attack on school indoctrination as engendering "obedience, docility, submission and passivity" (cited in Salter, 1995:4); (2) in contradistinction, a rival educational philosophy that argued that the schools should be primarily concerned with "life adjustment"; (3) the professionalization of the social sciences and the resulting conviction of many trained in these disciplines that their proper role was that of objective scientist, not that of uncritical supporter of the existing order; (4) the Great Depression, which led many intellectuals to consider alternative political models, especially socialism as presumably practiced in the grossly misunderstood and idealized Soviet Union; and (5) in the second half of the century, the corrosive consequences of Vietnam, the cold war, and Watergate.

36. For the effect of the Vietnam era on the baby boomers' political beliefs, see Delli Carpini (1986).

37. "There are influential educators today . . . who believe that the purpose of American education is to instill in children a pride in their ancestral pasts. [As a result, the teaching of] American history has become a pageant of exemplary slaves and black educators. Gay studies, women's studies, ethnic studies—the new curriculum ensures that education will be flattering" (Rodriguez, 1981:154–155).

38. For one thoughtful effort to explore multiculturalism and the problem of particularism, see Parens (1994).

39. We have understated the situation. Surveying civic education in the United States, Mary Jane Turner identified twelve "new approaches to political education." She awarded multicultural education, described quite favorably, "first position" (1981:62–64).

40. Other potential strategies exist beyond indoctrination through the education system. One strategy, based upon literature on preconditions for democracy, addresses the simple fact that Americans are enmeshed in authoritarian structures every day of their lives—and then expected to behave as virtuous democratic citizens when it comes to the world of government. If people are expected to be subservient in schools (students), in the workplace (employees), in the family, in social groups, and so on, this undermines the idea of equality and the sense of personal empowerment that are needed for democracy to exist.

To create a more democratic personality, we would have to consciously try to structure institutions of daily life to empower people. Evidence suggests that the more people become involved in high-school governance, workplace decisions, places of worship, and so on, the more apt they are to behave more vigorously and effectively in the world of governmental politics (e.g., Almond and Verba [1963]; Beck and Jennings, [1982]; Dahl [1970]; Peterson [1992]).

However, while we are not overly optimistic about the odds of successfully implementing the education reforms that we suggest, we believe that it is utopian to expect the American system to explicitly address empowering its citizens in all aspects of their lives. Thus we pursue this line of inquiry no further here, despite its obvious importance.

41. In essence, we are arguing for what Antonio Gramsci (1957) called a democratic "hegemony"—the inculcation of a common set of democratic values and norms—in *The Modern Prince and Other Writings*.

42. The several states, of course, normally delegate this responsibility to local governments, to school districts, and so forth.

43. Noting that graduation tests and teacher certification have been found to be associated with improved student performance, Smith and Meier (1995:329–343) suggest that the task is not completely hopeless. See also the effective-schools literature, e.g., Bickel (1990), Purkey and Smith (1983). The literature on school choice is relevant as well (e.g., Chubb and Moe, 1990).

Epilogue

Proponents of predictably unpopular ideas are usually well advised to be cautious in advancing their views, especially when these run counter to widely held and deeply cherished political beliefs. In such a situation, the danger is not so much that their beliefs will be summarily rejected but, rather, that they will be misunderstood—and then rejected. To preclude, or perhaps only to minimize the likelihood of such an eventuality, we should repeat a caveat voiced early in this volume.

Our primary objective in this book has been to explain the predominance of authoritarian governments and the relative rarity of democratic ones in human history. This striking disparity stems in large part, we have argued, from our species' evolutionary past. We are social primates, and hierarchical social structures, together with dominance, obedience, and other related behaviors, served a very useful purpose in furthering inclusive fitness among the social primates.

As a consequence, tendencies toward these structures and behaviors became an integral aspect of Homo sapiens' genetic legacy. Although still almost totally ignored in contemporary discussions of democratic theory and practice, these innate authoritarian predilections must be taken into consideration when we cast about for policies intended to strengthen and even expand governance.

That does not mean, however, that all of our political actions are determined by that legacy. Our species is unique in that acquired ideas and beliefs also profoundly influence what we do or do not do—and their influence is sometimes powerful enough to compel behaviors demonstrably different from those to which humankind would normally be inclined. In fact, were this not the case, democracies would not be so much uncommon as probably totally unknown.

Homo sapiens' social and political behavior is thus a function of the interplay between nurture and nature. For this reason, an explanation cast in purely evolutionary terms would be as seriously mistaken as the tabula rasa perspective, which looks solely at social conditioning, a perspective that has dominated the social and behavioral sciences for most of the twentieth century. Our desire here is to redress the balance, not to replace one grave misconception with another.

References

Aldendorfer, Mark. (1993). "Ritual, Hierarchy, and Change in Foraging Societies." *Journal of Anthropology and Archeology* 12: 1–40.

Alexander, Richard D. (1979). "Evolution and Culture." In Napoleon A. Chagnon and William Irons, eds., *Evolutionary Biology and Human Social Behavior*. North Scituate, MA: Duxbury Press.

———. (1987). *The Biology of Moral Systems*. New York: Aldine de Gruyter.

Allison, Graham T., Jr., and Robert P. Beschel, Jr. (1992). "Can the United States Promote Democracy?" *Political Science Quarterly* 107: 81–98.

Almond, Gabriel, and Sidney Verba. (1963). *The Civic Culture*. Boston: Little, Brown.

"Another Chapter of Justice." (1995). *The Economist* (June 16): 41–42.

Ansolabehere, Stephen, Shanto Iyengar, Adam Simon, and Nicholas Valentino. (1994). "Does Attack Advertising Demobilize the Electorate?" *American Political Science Review* 88: 829–838.

"Antigua's Old Man Passes on His Perch." (1994). *The Economist* (March 11): 46.

Arendt, Hannah. (1966). *Origins of Totalitarianism*. New York: Harcourt, Brace & World.

"The Army Learns of Human Rights." (1993). *The Economist* (October 22): 49.

Asch, Solomon. (1956). "Studies of Independence and Conformity: A Minority of One Against a Unanimous Majority." *Psychological Monographs* 70, no. 9.

"Back to Work." (1995). *The Economist* (May 26): 42.

Banks, Arthur S. (1972). "Correlates of Democratic Performance." *Comparative Politics* 4: 217–230.

Barash, David P. (1979). *The Whisperings Within: Evolution and the Origin of Human Nature*. New York: Harper & Row.

———. (1982). *Sociobiology and Behavior*. 2nd ed. New York: Elsevier.

———. (1986). *The Hare and the Tortoise*. New York: Viking.

———. (1994). "State Behavior, Individual Behavior, and the Legacy of Biology in a Troublesome World." *Politics and the Life Sciences* 13: 15–16.

Barkow, Jerome. (1989). *Darwin, Sex, and Status*. Toronto: University of Toronto Press.

Barner-Barry, Carol. (1977). "An Observational Study of Authority in a Preschool Peer Group." *Political Methodology* 4: 415–449.

———. (1981). "A Longitudinal Analysis of the Stability of Group Authority Structure." Paper presented at Western Political Science Association, Denver, Colorado.

Barro, Robert, and Xavier Saint Martin. (1995). *Economic Growth*. New York: McGraw-Hill.

Bauers, K. A., and J. P. Hearn. (1994). "Patterns of Paternity in Relation to Male Social Rank in the Stumptailed Macaque." *Behaviour* 129: 149–171.

Beck, Paul A., and M. Kent Jennings. (1982). "Pathways to Participation." *American Political Science Review* 76: 94–108.

Beer, Samuel. (1986). "The Rule of the Wise and Holy Hierarchy in the Thomistic System." *Political Theory* 14: 391–422.

Ben-Zvi, Abraham. (1994). *The United States and Israel*. New York: Columbia University Press.

Berelson, Bernard, and Gary A. Steiner. (1964). *Human Behavior: An Inventory of Scientific Findings*. New York: Harcourt.

Berline, David C., and Bruce J. Biddle. (1997). *The Manufactured Crisis: Myths, Fraud and the Attack on America's Public Schools*. White Plains, NY: Longman.

Berman, Carol M. (1986). "Maternal Lineages as Tools for Understanding Infant Social Development and Social Structure." In Richard G. Rawlins and Matt J. Kessler, eds., *The Cayo Santiago Macaques*. Albany: State University of New York Press.

Bernstein, Irwin S. (1981). "Dominance: The Baby and the Bathwater." *Behavioral and Brain Sciences* 4: 419–429.

Berreman, Gerald D. (1981). *Social Inequality: A Cross-Cultural Analysis*. New York: Academic Press.

Beteille, Andre. (1969). "The Decline in Social Inequality?" In Andre Beteille, ed., *Social Inequality: Selected Readings*. Baltimore: Penguin Books.

———. (1977). *Inequality among Men*. Delhi: Oxford University Press.

Betzig, Laura. (1986). *Despotism and Differential Reproduction*. New York: Aldine de Gruyter.

"Bhutto Claims Victory." (1993). *The Economist* (October 15): 31.

Bickel, William E. (1990). "The Effective Schools Literature: Implications for Research and Practice." In Terry B. Gutkin and Cecil R. Reynolds, eds., *The Handbook of School Psychology*. New York: Wiley.

Bishop, Charles D. (1989). "Comment on Headland and Reid." *Current Anthropology* 30: 52–54.

Bobbio, Norberto. (1987). *The Future of Democracy: A Defense of the Rules of the Game*. Minneapolis: University of Minnesota Press.

Boehm, C. (1984). "Can Social Hierarchy and Egalitarianism Both Be Ascribed to the Same Causal Forces?" *Politics and the Life Sciences* 3: 12–14.

———. (1993). "Egalitarian Behavior and Reverse Dominance Hierarchy." *Current Anthropology* 34: 227–254.

Bollen, Kenneth. (1991). "Political Democracy: Conceptual and Measurement Traps." In Alex Inkeles, ed., *On Measuring Democracy*. New Brunswick, NJ: Transaction.

———. (1993). "Liberal Democracy: Validity and Method Factors in Cross-National Measures." *American Journal of Political Science* 37: 1207–1230.

Brady, Frank, and F. A. Pottle, eds. (1995). *Boswell on the Grand Tour*. London: William Heinemann Ltd.

Brady, Henry E., Sidney Verba, and Kay Lehman Schlozman. (1995). "Beyond SES: A Resource Model of Political Participation." *American Political Science Review* 89: 271–294.

Brandon, Robert N. (1988). "The Levels of Selection: A Hierarchy of Interactors." In H. C. Plotkin, ed., *The Role of Behavior in Evolution*. Cambridge, MA: M.I.T. Press.

Bryce, James. (1921). *Modern Democracies*. London: Macmillan.

Burkhart, Ross E., and Michael S. Lewis-Beck. (1994). "Comparative Democracy: The Economic Development Thesis." *American Political Science Review* 88: 903–910.

"By Jingo." (1995). *The Economist* (October 13): 61–62.

Byrne, Richard W., and Andrew White, eds. (1988). *Machiavellian Intelligence*. Oxford: Clarendon Press.

Caton, Hiram. (1995). "Indoctrinability and Politics." Paper presented at the Symposium on Ideology and Indoctrinability, Andechs, Germany.

Chambliss, Rollin C. (1954). *Social Thought*. New York: Holt, Rinehart & Winston.

Cheney, Lynne V. (1990). *Tyrannical Machines: A Report on Educational Practices Gone Wrong and Our Best Hopes for Setting Them Right*. Washington, DC: National Endowment for the Humanities.

Chirot, Daniel. (1994). *Modern Tyrants*. New York: Free Press.

Chomsky, Noam. (1972). *Language and Mind*. 2nd ed. New York: Harcourt Brace Jovanovich.

Chubb, John E., and Terry M. Moe. (1990). *Politics, Markets and America's Schools*. Washington, DC: Brookings Institution.

"The Civilian Emperor." (1995). *The Economist* (June 9): 8–10.

"Congress Takes Its Own Lid Off." (1994). *The Economist* (February 4): 48.

Coppedge, Michael, and Wolfgang H. Reinicke. (1991). "Measuring Polyarchy." In Alex Inkeles, ed., *On Measuring Democracy*. New Brunswick, NJ: Transaction.

Crick, Bernard. (1960). *The American Science of Politics*. Berkeley: University of California Press.

Cutright, Philips. (1963). "National Political Development: Measurement and Analysis." *American Sociological Review* 28: 253–264.

Dahl, Robert A. (1956). *A Preface to Democratic Theory*. Chicago: University of Chicago Press.

———. (1970). *After the Revolution?* New Haven: Yale University Press.

———. (1971). *Polyarchy*. New Haven: Yale University Press.

———. (1989). *Democracy and Its Critics*. New Haven: Yale University Press.

———. (1991). *Modern Political Analysis*. Englewood Cliffs, NJ: Prentice Hall, 1991.

Dahrendorf, Ralf. (1968). *Essays on the Theory of Society*. Stanford: Stanford University Press.

Davis, R. W., ed. (1995). *The Origins of Modern Freedom in the West*. Stanford: Stanford University Press.

Dawkins, Richard. (1989a). *The Extended Phenotype*. Oxford: Oxford University Press.

———. (1989b). *The Selfish Gene*. 2nd edition. New York: Oxford University Press.

———. (1993). "Is God a Computer Virus?" In B. Dahlbom, ed., *Dennett and His Critics: Demystifying the Mind*. London: Basil Blackwell.

Degler, Carl. (1991). *In Search of Human Nature*. New York: Oxford University Press.

Delli Carpini, Michael X. (1986). *Stability and Change in American Politics.* New York: New York University Press.

"Democracy and Growth." (1994). *The Economist* (August 27): 15–17.

de Ruiter, J. R., Jon A.R.A.M. van Hooff, and W. Scheffrahn. (1993). "Social and Genetic Aspects of Paternity in Wild Long-tailed Macaques." *Behaviour* 129: 203–224.

de Tocqueville, Alexis. (1945). *Democracy in America.* Books 1, 2, 3, and 4. New York: Knopf.

Deutsch, Karl W. (1961). "Social Mobilization and Political Development." *American Political Science Review* 55: 493–514.

de Waal, Frans. (1989). *Peacemaking among Primates.* Cambridge, MA: Harvard University Press.

Diamond, Larry, Juan Linz, and Seymour Martin Lipset. (1990). *Democracy in Developing Countries, 1988–1989.* New York: Lynne Reiner.

Dionne, E. J. (1991). *Why Americans Hate Politics.* New York: Simon & Schuster.

DiPalma, Giuseppe. (1990). *To Craft Democracies.* Berkeley: University of California Press.

"The Distant Sound of Rattling Sabres." (1994). *The Economist* (April 15): 37.

Dixon, William J. (1994). "Democracy and the Peaceful Settlement of International Conflict." *American Political Science Review* 88: 14–32.

Dixson, A. F., T. Bossi, and E. J. Wickings. (1993). "Male Dominance and Genetically Determined Reproductive Success in the Mandrill." *Primates* 34: 525–532.

Dolgoff, Sam, ed. (1974). *The Anarchist Collectives.* New York: Free Life Editions.

Dostoyevsky, Fyodor. (1957). *The Brothers Karamazov.* Translated by Constance Garnett. New York: New American Library.

Du Gard, Martin. (1972). *Jean Barois.* Paris: Gallimard.

Dumont, Louis. (1966). *Homo Hierarchicus.* Chicago: University of Chicago Press.

Easton, David. (1956). *A Framework for Political Analysis.* Englewood Cliffs, NJ: Prentice Hall.

Eaton, G. Gray. (1976). "The Social Order of Japanese Macaques." *Scientific American* 235: 97–106.

Edelman, Murray S., and Donald R. Omark. (1973). "Dominance and Hierarchies in Young Children." *Social Science Information* 12: 103–110.

Eibl-Eibesfeldt, Irenaus. (1979). "Human Ethology" With accompanying commentaries. *The Behavioral and Brain Sciences* 2: 1–57.

———. (1982). "Warfare, Man's Indoctrinability, and Group Selection." *Zeitschrift für Tierpsychologie* 60: 177–198.

———. (1989). *Human Ethology.* New York: Aldine de Gruyter.

Ellis, Lee. (1993). "Operationally Defining Social Stratification in Human and Nonhuman Animals." In Lee Ellis, ed., *Stratification and Socioeconomic Inequality, Vol. I.* Westport, CT: Praeger.

———. (1995). "Dominance and Reproductive Success among Nonhuman Animals: A Cross-species Comparison." *Ethology and Sociobiology* 16: 257–333.

Elshtain, Jean Bethke. (1995). *Democracy on Trial.* New York: Basic Books.

Ely, J., P. Alford, and R. E. Ferrell. (1991). "DNA 'Fingerprinting' and the Genetic Management of a Captive Chimpanzee Population." *American Journal of Primatology* 24: 39–54.

Etzioni, Amitai. (1993). *The Spirit of Community.* New York: Crown.

"The Fading of the Red." (1994). *The Economist* (January 21): 56.

Fallows, James. (1996). *Breaking the News: How the Media Undermine American Democracy*. New York: Pantheon.

Farrar, Cynthia. (1988). *The Origins of Democratic Thinking*. New York: Cambridge University Press.

Flanagan, J. (1989). "Hierarchy in Simple 'Egalitarian' Societies." *Annual Review of Anthropology* 18: 245–266.

Foley, R. A., ed. (1991). *Origins of Human Behavior*. London: Unwin Hyman.

Fox, Robin. (1989). *The Search for Society*. New Brunswick, NJ: Rutgers University Press.

Frank, Jerome. (1944). "Experimental Studies of Personal Pressure and Resistance." *Journal of Genetic Psychology* 30: 23–64.

Frank, Robert H. (1985). *Choosing the Right Pond: Human Behavior and the Search for Status*. New York: Oxford University Press.

Fromm, Eric. (1941). *Escape from Freedom*. New York: Farrar and Richard.

"Fujimoriland." (1994). *The Economist* (May 13): 48.

Gardner, Peter M. (1991). "Foragers' Pursuit of Individual Autonomy." *Current Anthropology* 32: 543–572.

Gasiorowski, Mark J. (1995). "Economic Crisis and Political Regime Change: An Event History Analysis." *American Political Science Review* 89: 882–897.

Gastil, Raymond Duncan. (1989). *Freedom in the World*. New York: Freedom House.

———. (1991). "The Comparative Survey of Freedom." In Alex Inkeles, ed., *On Measuring Democracy*. New Brunswick, NJ: Transaction.

Gellner, E. (1980). *Soviet and Western Anthropology*. London: Duckworth.

"Getting It Right." (1994). *The Economist* (June 3): 48–49.

Gibson, James L. (1988). "Political Intolerance and Political Repression during the McCarthy Red Scare." *American Political Science Review* 82: 511–529.

Ginsberg, Benjamin. (1986). *The Captive Public: How Mass Opinion Promotes State Power*. New York: Basic Books.

Ginsburg, Benson E. (1988). "The Evolution of Social and Political Behavior." Presented at American Political Science Association, Washington, D. C.

"Glimmering Path." (1995). *The Economist* (August 4): 30–31.

Goldberg, Steven. (1993). *Why Men Rule*. Chicago: Open Court Press.

Gordon, Robert. (1992). *The Bushman Myth*. Boulder, CO: Westview Press.

Gould, Stephen J. (1992). "Punctuated Equilibrium in Fact and in Theory." In Albert Somit and Steven A. Peterson, eds., *The Dynamics of Evolution*. Ithaca, NY: Cornell University Press.

Gramsci, Antonio. (1957). *The Modern Prince and Other Writings*. (Translated by Louis Marks). New York: International Publishers.

Greider, William. (1992). *Who Will Tell the People? The Betrayal of American Democracy*. New York: Simon & Schuster.

"Guns and Votes." (1995). *The Economist* (August 11): 32.

Gurr, Ted Robert. (1974). "Persistence and Change in Political Systems, 1800–1971." *American Political Science Review* 68: 1482–1504.

Hall, K.R.L., and Irven DeVore. (1965). "Baboon Social Behavior." In Irven DeVore, ed., *Primate Behavior*. New York: Holt, Rinehart, & Winston.

Hanson, Russell L. (1985). *The Democratic Imagination in America*. Princeton: Princeton University Press.

Harcourt, A. H., and Frans de Waal, eds. (1992). *Coalitions and Alliances in Humans and Other Animals*. New York: Oxford University Press.

Harff, Barbara, and Ted Robert Gurr. (1995). "Victims of the State: Genocides, Politicides and Group Repression from 1945 to 1995." *PIOOM Newsletter and Progress Report* 7 (Winter): 24–39.

Hausfater, Glenn, Jeanne Altmann, and Stuart Altmann. (1982). "Long-term Consistency of Dominance Relations among Female Baboons (*Papio Cynocephalus*)." *Science* 217: 752–755.

Havel, Vaclav. (1987). *Vaclav Havel, or, Living in Truth.* Boston: Faber & Faber.

———. (1990). *Disturbing the Peace.* New York: Knopf.

Hazarika, Sanjay. (1994). "India's Newest Hero Makes Elections Fair Again." *New York Times* (January 30): 9.

Headland, Thomas N., and Lawrence A. Reid. (1989). "Hunter-Gatherers and Their Neighbors from Prehistory to the Present." *Current Anthropology* 30: 43–66.

Held, David. (1993). "Democracy: From City-States to a Cosmopolitan Order?" In David Held, ed., *Prospects for Democracy.* Stanford: Stanford University Press.

Hendricks, J. W. (1988). "Power and Knowledge: Discourse and Ideological Transformation among the Shuar." *American Ethnologist* 15: 216–238.

Hepburn, Mary A. (1990). "Educating for Democracy: The Years Following World War II." *The Social Studies* (July–August): 153–160.

Herrnstein, Richard J., and Charles Murray. (1994). *The Bell Curve.* New York: The Free Press.

Hofling, C. K., et al. (1966). "An Experimental Study of Nurse-Physician Relations." *Journal of Nervous and Mental Disease* 143: 171–180.

Hold, B. (1977). "Attention Structure and Rank-Specific Behavior in Preschool Children." In M.R.A. Chance and R. R. Larsen, eds., *The Social Structure of Attention.* New York: Wiley.

———. (1980). "Attention Structure and Behavior in San Children." *Ethology and Sociobiology* 1: 275–290.

Holden, Constance. (1995). "Alabama Schools Disclaim Evolution," *Science,* 270: 1305.

"Hucksters on the Hustings." (1995). *The Economist* (June 30): 36.

Huntington, Samuel P. (1991). *The Third Wave.* Norman: University of Oklahoma Press.

———. (1991–1992). "How Countries Democratize." *Political Science Quarterly* 106: 579–616.

Inglehart, Ronald. (1990). *Culture Shift.* Princeton: Princeton University Press.

Ingold, Tim, David Riches, and James Woodburn. (1988). *Hunters and Gatherers.* New York: Oxford University Press.

"In Manila, the Film Makers Test the Censors." (1994). *New York Times* (March 27): 14.

Jacoby, Russell. (1994). *Dogmatic Wisdom: How the Culture Wars Have Misled America.* New York: Doubleday.

Jolly, Alison. (1985). *The Evolution of Primate Behavior.* 2nd ed. New York: Macmillan.

Jones, A.H.M. (1940). *The Greek City from Alexander to Justinian.* London: Oxford.

Jones, Steve. (1994). *The Language of Genes.* New York: HarperCollins.

"Just for Show." (1994). *The Economist* (April 15): 53.

Karatnycky, Adrian. (1996). "Democracy and Despotism: Bipolarism Renewed?" *Freedom Review* 27 (January–February): 1–16.

Kaus, Mickey. (1992). *The End of Equality.* New York: Basic Books.

Keeley, Lawrence N. (1996). *War before Civilization: The Myth of the Peaceful Savage.* Oxford: Oxford University Press.

Kelly, Kevin. (1994). *The Rise of Neo Biological Civilization.* Reading, MA: Addison-Wesley.

Kelman, Herbert C. and V. L. Hamilton. (1989). *Crimes of Obedience.* New Haven: Yale University Press.

Key, V. O., Jr. (1949). *Southern Politics.* New York: Vintage Books.

Kilham, W., and L. Mann. (1974). "Level of Destructive Obedience as a Function of Transmitter and Executant Roles in the Milgram Obedience Paradigm." *Journal of Personality and Social Psychology* 29: 696–702.

Kingdon, Jonathan. (1993). *Self-Made Man: Evolution from Eden.* New York: Wiley.

Knauft, Bruce M. (1991). "Violence and Sociality in Human Evolution." *Current Anthropology* 32: 391–428.

Koford, Carl. (1963). "Group Relations in an Island Colony of Rhesus Macaques." In Charles Southwick, ed., *Primate Social Relations.* Princeton: D. Van Nostrand.

Lasch, Christopher. (1995). *The Revolt of the Elites and the Betrayal of Democracy.* New York: Norton.

Lasswell, Harold D., and Nathan Leites, eds. (1949). *Language of Politics.* Cambridge, MA: M.I.T. Press.

"Latin America's Freeish Press." (1995). *The Economist* (May 19): 46.

Layton, Robert, et al. (1991). "The Transition between Hunting and Gathering and the Specialized Husbandry of Resources." *Current Anthropology* 32: 255–274.

Leacock, Eleanor B., and Richard Lee, eds. (1982). *Politics and History in Band Society.* Cambridge: Cambridge University Press.

Leakey, Richard, and Roger Lewin. (1992). *Origins Reconsidered.* New York: Doubleday.

Lee, Richard B., and Irven DeVore, eds. (1968). *Man the Hunter.* Chicago: Aldine.

Lerner, Daniel. (1958). *The Passing of Traditional Society.* New York: The Free Press.

Levinton, Jeffrey. (1988). *Genetics, Paleontology, and Macroevolution.* Cambridge: Cambridge University Press.

Linz, Juan. (1978). *The Breakdown of Democratic Regimes.* Baltimore: The Johns Hopkins Press.

Lipset, Seymour Martin. (1963). *Political Man.* Garden City, NY: Anchor Books.

———. (1995). "Malaise and Resiliency in America." *Journal of Democracy* 6: 6–18.

Lockard, Joan, ed. (1980). *The Evolution of Human Social Behavior.* New York: Elsevier.

Lorenz, Konrad Z. (1966). *On Aggression.* New York: Harcourt Brace Jovanovich.

McColm, R. B. (1991). "The Comparative Survey of Freedom: 1991." *Freedom Review* 221: 5–24.

McCrone, Donald J., and Charles F. Cnudde. (1967). "Toward a Communications Theory of Democratic Development." *American Political Science Review* 61: 72–79.

McDonald, Dwight. (1974). *Discriminations.* New York: Viking.

McGuinness, Diane, ed. (1987). *Dominance, Aggression, and War.* New York: Paragon House.

McNamara, Robert S. (1995). *In Retrospect.* New York: Random House.

Madrick, Jeffrey. (1995). *The End of Affluence: The Cause and Consequences of America's Economic Decline.* New York: Random House.

Mansbridge, Jane J. (1980). *Beyond Adversary Democracy.* New York: Basic Books.

Mantell, David M. (1971). "The Potential for Violence in Germany." *Journal of Social Issues* 27: 101–112.

Maoz, Zeev, and Bruce Russett. (1993). "Normative and Structural Causes of Democratic Peace, 1946–1986." *American Political Science Review* 87: 624–638.

Martin, John, et al. (1976). "Obedience under Conditions Demanding Self-Immolation." *Human Relations* 29: 345–356.

Maynard-Smith, J. (1982). *Evolution and the Theory of Games*. Cambridge: Cambridge University Press.

Mayo, H. B. (1960). *An Introduction to Democratic Theory*. New York: Oxford University Press.

Mayr, Ernst. (1970). *Populations, Species, and Evolution*. Cambridge, MA: Harvard University Press.

Meeus, W. H., and Q.A.W. Raaijmakers. (1985). "Administrative Obedience." Unpublished manuscript cited in Miller (1986).

Meillassoux, C. (1973). "On the Mode of Production of the Hunting Band." In Pierre Alexandre, ed., *French Perspectives in African Studies*. London: Oxford University Press for the International African Institute.

Merritt, Richard L., and Dina Zinnes. (1991). "Democracies and War." In Alex Inkeles, ed., *On Measuring Democracy*. New Brunswick, NJ: Transaction.

Michels, Roberto. (1915). *Political Parties*. Glencoe, IL: Free Press.

Michnik, Adam. (1986). *Letters from Prison*. Berkeley: University of California Press.

Milgram, Stanley. (1974). *Obedience to Authority: An Experimental View*. New York: Harper & Row.

Miller, Arthur G. (1986). *The Obedience Experiments*. New York: Praeger.

Milton, John. (1992). "Aeropagitica." In Diane Ravitch and Abigail Thernstrom, eds., *The Democracy Reader*. New York: HarperCollins.

Moore, Barrington. (1978). *Injustice: The Social Bases of Obedience and Revolt*. White Plains, NY: Sharpe.

"More Cash than Dash." (1995). *The Economist* (June 2): 34, 36.

Morley, David. (1994). "The Rules in the Dominican Republic." *The Globe and Mail* (August 5): A19.

Mosca, Gaetano. (1939). *The Ruling Class*. Translated by Hannah D. Kahn. New York: McGraw-Hill.

Moyer, K. E. (1987). "The Biological Basis of Dominance and Aggression. In Diane McGuinness, ed., *Dominance, Aggression, and War*. New York: Paragon House.

Muller, Edward N. (1988). "Democracy, Economic Development, and Income Inequality." *American Sociological Review* 53: 50–68.

Muller, Edward N., and Mitchell A. Seligson. (1994). "Civic Culture and Democracy." *American Political Science Review* 88: 635–652.

"Muzzling the Press." (1995). *The Economist* (October 6): 36.

Myers, F. R. (1988). "Critical Trends in the Study of Hunter-Gatherers." *Annual Review of Anthropology* 17: 261–282.

National Commission on Excellence in Education. (1983). *A Nation at Risk*. Washington, DC: Government Printing Office.

"National Insecurity." (1994). *The Economist* (May 20): 38.

Nelson, Daniel N., and Samuel Bentley. (1994). "The Comparative Politics of Eastern Europe." *PS* 27: 45–52.

Nesse, Randolph N. (1994). "An Evolutionary Perspective on Substance Abuse." *Ethology and Sociobiology* 15: 339–348.

Neubauer, Deane E. (1967). "Some Conditions of Democracy." *American Political Science Review* 61: 1002–1009.

"New Politricks." (1995). *The Economist* (October 13).

"Not So Militant." (1995). *The Economist* (June 16): 35.

Ober, Josiah. (1993). "Public Speech and the Power of the People in Democratic Athens." *PS* 26: 481–486.

O'Brien, Conor Cruise. (1991). "Nationalists and Democrats." *New York Review of Books* (August 15): 29–31.

O'Donnell, Guillermo A. (1973). *Modernization and Bureaucratic Authoritarianism.* Berkeley: University of California Press.

Oldenburg, Ray. (1989). *The Great Good Place.* New York: Paragon House.

Omark, D. R., and M. S. Edelman. (1975). "A Comparison of Status Hierarchies in Young Children." *Social Science Information* 14: 87–107.

"One Law for the Lawmakers." (1993). *The Economist* (December 10): 50.

Packer, C., D. A. Collins, A. Sindimovo, and Jane Goodall. (1995). "Reproductive Constraints on Aggressive Competition in Female Baboons." *Nature* 373: 60–63.

Page, Benjamin I., and Robert Y. Shapiro. (1992). *The Rational Public.* Chicago: University of Chicago Press.

Pagels, Elaine. (1979). *The Gnostic Gospels.* New York: Random House.

Parens, Joshua. (1994). "Multiculturalism and the Problem of Particularism." *American Political Science Review* 88: 169–181.

Pareto, Vilfredo. (1935). *The Mind and Society.* Edited by Arthur Livingston. New York: Harcourt Brace Jovanovich.

Patkar, Vivek. (1993). "On the Conservation of Human Suffering." *Journal of Social and Evolutionary Systems* 16: 1–7.

Paul, A., and J. Kuester. (1990). "Adaptive Significance of Sex Ratio Adjustment in Semifree-Ranging Barbary Macaques at Salem." *Behavioral Ecology and Sociobiology* 27: 287–293.

Paul, A., J. Kuester, A. Timme, and J. Arnemann. (1993). "The Association between Rank, Mating Effort, and Reproductive Success in Male Barbary Macaques." *Primates* 34: 491–502.

Peterson, Steven A. (1990). *Political Behavior: Patterns in Everyday Life.* Beverly Hills: Sage.

———. (1992). "Church Participation and Political Participation: The Spillover Effect." *American Politics Quarterly* 20: 123–139.

Phillips, Kevin P. (1990). *Politics of Rich and Poor.* New York: Random House.

Pickert, S. M., and S. J. Wall. (1981). "An Investigation of Children's Perspectives of Dominance Relations." *Perceptual and Motor Skills* 52: 75–81.

Plano, Jack C., and Milton Greenberg. (1993). *The American Political Dictionary.* 9th ed. Fort Worth: Harcourt Brace Jovanovich.

Plotkin, H. C., ed. (1988). *The Role of Behavior in Evolution.* Cambridge, MA: M.I.T. Press.

"Politics versus Policy." (1994). *The Economist* (April 22): 9.

Potter, David. (1993). "Democratization in Asia." In David Held, ed., *Prospects for Democracy.* Stanford: Stanford University Press.

Purkey, Stewart C., and Marshall S. Smith. (1983). "Effective Schools: A Review." *The Elementary School Journal* 83: 427–452.

Putnam, Robert D. (1995a). "Bowling Alone: America's Declining Social Capital." *Journal of Democracy* 6: 65–78.

———. (1995b). "Tuning In, Tuning Out: The Strange Disappearance of Social Capital in America." *PS* 28: 664–683.

Putnam, Robert D., Robert Leonardi, and Raffaella Nanetti. (1993). *Making Democracy Work: Civic Tradition in Modern Italy.* Princeton: Princeton University Press.

Rank, S. G., and C. K. Jacobson. (1977). "Hospital Nurses' Compliance with Medication Overdose Orders." *Journal of Health and Social Behavior* 18: 188–193.

Raywid, Mary Anne. (1980). "The Discovery and Rejection of Indoctrination." *Educational Theory* 30, no. 1: 1–10.

Reich, Robert B. (1992). *The Work of Nations.* New York: Random House.

"Reviving Death." (1993). *The Economist* (December 24): 33.

"The Revolt of the Indian Judges." (1993). *The Economist* (October 22): 36.

Reynolds, Peter. (1987). *Political Economy.* New York: St. Martin's.

Ridley, Matt. (1994). *The Red Queen.* New York: Viking.

Rodriguez, Richard. (1981). *Hunger of Memory: The Education of Richard Rodriguez.* Boston: D. R. Godine.

Rohter, Larry. (1994). "Campaign in Bahamas Forces Haitians to Flee for the U.S." *New York Times* (January 2): 1.

Rokeach, Milton. (1960). *The Open and Closed Mind.* New York: Basic Books.

"Rotten Politicians for Rotten Voters." (1994). *The Economist* (January 14): 37.

"Rougher Road." (1994). *The Economist* (June 25): 42.

Rousseau, Jean-Jacques. (1973). Translated by G.D.H. Cole. *The Social Contract.* Books 1, 2, 3, and 4. London: Dent.

Ruse, Michael. (1986). *Taking Darwin Seriously.* New York: Blackwell.

Russett, Bruce. (1993). *Grasping the Democratic Peace.* Princeton: Princeton University Press.

Russett, Bruce, and William Antholis. (1992). "Do Democracies Rarely Fight Each Other? Evidence from the Peloponnesian War." *Journal of Peace Research* 29: 415–434.

Rustow, Alexander. (1980). *Freedom and Domination.* Translated by Salvator Attanasio. Princeton: Princeton University Press.

Rustow, Dankwart. (1970). "Transition to Democracy." *Comparative Politics* 2: 337–364.

Sagan, Carl, and Ann Druyan. (1992). *Shadows of Forgotten Ancestors.* New York: Ballantine Books.

Sahlins, Marshall D. (1958). *Social Stratification in Polynesia.* Seattle: University of Washington Press.

Salter, Frank. (1995). "Indoctrination as Institutionalized Persuasion." Paper presented at Symposium on Warfare, Ideology, and Indoctrinability, Ringberg Castle, Germany.

Samuelson, Robert J. (1996). *The Age of Entitlement: How the American Dream Became the American Fantasy.* New York: Random House.

Sartori, Giovanni. (1965). *Democratic Theory.* 2nd ed. New York: Praeger.

Schoultz, Lars, William C. Smith, and Augustus Varos. (1994). *Security, Democracy, and Development in U.S.–Latin American Relations.* Miami: University of Miami.

Schwartz, Peter H. (1989). "'His Majesty the Baby': Narcissism and Royal Authority." *Political Theory* 17: 266–290.

Scott, John Paul, and Benson E. Ginsburg. (1994). "The Seville Statement on Violence Revisited." *American Psychologist* 49: 849–850.

"Second Thoughts in Fiji." (1994). *The Economist* (March 11): 37.

"The Secret of Japan's Safe Streets." (1994). *The Economist* (April 22): 38.

Shack, W. A., and P. S. Cohen, eds. (1979). *Politics in Leadership*. Oxford: Clarendon Press.

Shanab, M. E., and K. A. Yahya. (1978). "A Cross-Cultural Study of Obedience." *Bulletin of the Psychonomic Society* 11: 267–269.

Shaw, R. Paul, and Yuwa Wong. (1989) *Genetic Seeds of Warfare*. Boston: Unwin Hyman.

Shepher, Joseph. (1987). "Commentary." In Diane McGuinness, ed., In *Dominance, Aggression and War*. New York: Paragon House.

Sheridan, C. L., and R. G. King. (1972). "Obedience to Authority with an Authentic Victim." *Proceedings of the American Psychological Association* (1972): 156–166.

Sherif, Muzafer. (1936). *The Psychology of Social Norms*. New York: Harper & Row.

Silberman, George. (1982). "Political Process in G/wi Bands." In E. B. Leacock and R. Lee, eds., *Politics and History in Band Society*. Cambridge: Cambridge University Press.

Simon, Herbert. (1990). "A Mechanism for Social Selection and Successful Altruism." *Science* 250: 1665–1668.

Simpson, George Gaylord. (1944). *Tempo and Mode*. New York: Columbia University Press.

———. (1953). *The Major Features of Evolution*. New York: Columbia University Press.

Sinnott, E. W. (1945). "The Biological Basis of Democracy." *Yale Review* 35: 61–73.

Skinner, B. F. (1971). *Beyond Freedom and Dignity*. New York: Knopf.

Sluckin, A. H., and D. R. Omark. (1973). "Dominance Hierarchies in Young Children." *Social Science Information* 12: 103–110.

Smith, D. G. (1993). "A 15-year Study of the Association between Dominance Rank and Reproductive Success of Male Rhesus Macaques." *Primates* 34: 471–480.

Smith, Kevin B., and Kenneth J. Meier. (1995). *The Case Against School Choice*. Armonk, NY: Sharpe.

Sorenson, Georg. (1993). *Democracy and Democratization*. Boulder, CO: Westview Press.

"South Korea's Local Heroes." (1995). *The Economist* (July 7): 25–26.

Staub, Ervin. (1989). *The Roots of Evil: The Origins of Genocide and Other Group Violence*. New York: Cambridge University Press.

Stayton, D. J., R. Hogan, and M. D. Ainsworth. (1971). "Infant Obedience and Maternal Behavior: The Origins of Socialization Reconsidered." *Child Development* 42: 1057–1069.

Steel, Ronald. (1995). *Temptations of a Superpower*. New York: Knopf.

Steinem, Gloria. (1992). *Revolution from Within*. Boston: Little, Brown.

Sterngold, James. (1994). "Japanese Begin to Crack the Wall of Secrecy around Official Acts." *New York Times* (May 15): 1.

Stewart, Kelly J., and Alexander H. Harcourt. (1987). "Gorillas: Variation in Female Relationships." In Barbara Smuts et al., eds., *Primate Societies*. Chicago: University of Chicago Press.

Strayer, F. F., and J. Strayer. (1976). "An Ethological Analysis of Social Agonism and Dominance Relations among Preschool Children." *Child Development* 47: 980–989.

Sullivan, John L., James Piereson, and George E. Marcus. (1982). *Political Tolerance and American Democracy*. Chicago: University of Chicago Press.

Sullivan, Michael J. (1992). "Democratic States in the 'Measuring Global Values' Comparative Government Spread Sheet." Paper presented at Northeastern Political Science Association meeting, Providence, Rhode Island.

Sykes, Charles J. (1996). *Dumbing Down Our Kids: Why American Children Feel Good About Themselves But Can't Read, Write, or Add.* New York: St. Martin's.

Tarrow, Sidney. (1996). "Making Social Science Work across Space and Time: A Critical Reflection on Robert Putnam's *Making Democracy Work.*" *American Political Science Review* 90: 389–397.

Tawney, R. H. (1931). *Equality.* New York: Harcourt Brace Jovanovich.

Testart, A. (1988). "Some Major Problems in the Social Anthropology of Hunter-Gatherers." *Current Anthropology* 29: 1–31.

"Thailand's Frail Democracy." (1995). *The Economist* (May 19): 15.

Tiger, Lionel. (1979). *Optimism: The Biology of Hope.* New York: Simon and Schuster.

———. (1992). *The Pursuit of Pleasure.* Boston: Little, Brown.

Tiger, Lionel, and Robin S. Fox. (1971). *The Imperial Animal.* New York: Dell.

"Trapped." (1995). *The Economist* (June 23): 38.

Trivers, Robert. (1971). "The Evolution of Reciprocal Altruism." *Quarterly Review of Biology* 46: 35–57.

———. (1972). "Parental Investment and Sexual Selection." In Bernard Campbell, ed., *Sexual Selection and the Descent of Man.* Chicago: Aldine.

———. (1974). Parent-Offspring Conflict." *American Zoologist* 14: 249–264.

Turner, Mary Jane. (1981). "Civic Education in the United States." In Derek Hester and Judith Gillespie, eds., *Political Education in Flux.* Beverly Hills: Sage.

Tyack, David, and Larry Cuban. (1995). *Tinkering Toward Utopia: A Century of Public School Reform.* Cambridge, MA: Harvard University Press.

Ulmer, M. D. (1987). "Fifty Years of Keynes." *The Public Interest* 87 (Spring): 110–117.

UNESCO. (1951). *Democracy in a World of Tensions.* Chicago: University of Chicago Press.

"Unsteady Mexico." (1994). *The Economist* (April 8): 15.

van den Berghe, Pierre L. (1980). "The Human Family." In Joan S. Lockard, ed., *The Evolution of Human Social Behavior.* New York: Elsevier.

van der Dennen, Johan, and Vincent Falger, eds. (1990). *Sociobiology and Conflict.* London: Chapman and Hall.

van der Molen, P. P. (1990). "The Biological Instability of Social Equilibria." In Johan van der Dennen and Vincent Falger, eds., *Sociobiology and Conflict.* London: Chapman and Hall.

Vanhanen, Tatu. (1984). *The Emergence of Democracy.* Helsinki: The Finnish Society of Sciences and Letters.

———. (1990). *The Process of Democratization.* New York: Crane Russak.

———. (1994). "Global Trends of Democratization in the 1990s: A Statistical Analysis." Paper presented at the International Political Science Association, Berlin.

"Venezuela Suspends Certain Rights, Imposes Currency and Price Controls." (1994). *The Wall Street Journal* (June 28): A14.

Wallerstein, Immanuel. (1974). "The Rise and Future Demise of the World-capitalist System." *Comparative Studies in Society and History* 16: 400–415.

Walters, Jeffrey R., and Robert M. Seyfarth. (1987). "Conflict and Cooperation." In Barbara Smuts et al., eds., *Primate Societies.* Chicago: University of Chicago Press.

Werlin, Herbert. (1994). "A Primary/Secondary Democracy Distinction." *PS* 28: 530–534.

Wilkinson, Rupert. (1969). *Governing Elites: Studies in Training and Selection*. Oxford: Oxford University Press.

Willhoite, Fred. (1975). "Equal Opportunity and Primate Particularism." *Journal of Politics* 37: 270–276.

Williams, George C. (1966). *Adaptation and Natural Selection*. Princeton: Princeton University Press.

Wilson, David Sloan. (1995). "Group Selection and Human Ethology." *Human Ethology Bulletin* 10, no. 3: 2–4.

Wilson, David Sloan and Elliott Sober. (1994). "Reintroducing Group Selection to the Human Behavioral Sciences." With accompanying commentaries. *Behavioral and Brain Sciences* 17: 585–654.

Wilson, Edward O. (1975). *Sociobiology*. Cambridge, MA: Harvard University Press.

———. (1978). *On Human Nature*. Cambridge, MA: Harvard University Press.

Woodburn, J. (1979). "Minimal Politics: The Political Organization of Hada." In W. A. Shack and P. S. Cohen, eds., *Politics in Leadership*. Oxford: Clarendon Press.

———. (1980). "Hunters and Gatherers Today and Reconstruction of the Past." In E. Gellner, ed., *Soviet and Western Anthropology*. London: Duckworth.

———. (1982). "Egalitarian Societies." *Man* 17: 431–451.

Wright, Robert. (1994). *The Moral Animal*. New York: Vintage Books.

Index

Alexander, Richard, 81, 99, 101, 117 n.5, 117 n.6
Aquinas, St. Thomas, 90
Ardrey, Robert, 117 n.7
Arendt, Hannah, 91, 96 n.16
Aristotle, 18, 60, 88
Asch, Solomon, 72
Athens, 34

Barash, David, 62 n.3, 67, 78, 82, 83 n.6
Beer, Samuel, 88
Berreman, Gerald D., 51
Beteille, Andre, 55
Betzig, Laura, 70
Bobbio, Norberto, 95 n.10
Bollen, Kenneth, 38
Brandon, Robert N., 80
Bryce, James, 89

Calvin, John, 60
Chomsky, Noam, 56
Churchill, Winston, 116 n.1
Cicero, 90
Comte, Auguste, 73
Counts, George, 115
Culture, 9–10

Dahl, Robert, 35, 36, 37, 38, 85, 86, 94 n.1, 94 n.3, 95 n.11
Dahrendorf, Ralf, 63 n.24, 68
Darwin, Charles, 14 n.8
Dawkins, Richard, 6, 99–100
Degler, Carl, 68, 74 n.3
Delayed return societies, 59
Delli Carpini, Michael X., 120 n.36
Democracy: ambiguity of term, 86, 89–94; causes of, 17–29; consensual, 38–39, 42–43; culture, 24–25; defined, 17, 32–34, 89–90; direct, 95 n.7; domestic policy and, 107–116; education and, 111–116; foreign policy and, 103–107; indoctrinability and, 110–116
Democratic centralism, 92–93
de Tocqueville, Alexis, 8, 14 n.6, 18, 24, 29 n.2, 30 n.9, 92–93
Dewey, John, 112, 115, 120 n.35
Dolgoff, Sam, 63 n.23
Dominance: alliances, 52–53, 54; defined, 52–53; evolutionary benefits of, 53–54; DuGard, Martin, 64 n.26
Dostoyevsky, Fyodor, 68, 74 n.10
DuGard, Martin, 64 n.26
Dumont, Louis, 56

Easton, David, 74 n.2

About the Authors

ALBERT SOMIT is Distinguished Service Professor Emeritus at Southern Illinois University. He has served as Executive Vice President of the State University of New York at Buffalo and President of Southern Illinois University. He is one of the pioneers in the field of biology and politics and the founder of the International Political Science Association Research Committee #12 (Biology and Politics). He has written or edited numerous works, the most relevant of which are *Biology and Politics: Recent Explorations* (1976), *The Dynamics of Evolution* (coedited with Steven A. Peterson), *Biopolitics and the Mainstream* (coedited with Peterson), and *Human Nature and Politics* (coedited with Joseph Losco).

STEVEN A. PETERSON is Professor of Political Science at Alfred University. He has been active in the Association for Politics and the Life Sciences and Research Committee #12 of the International Political Science Association. He has authored numerous articles in biology and politics as well as several books focusing on the subjects.